The Word *becoming* Flesh

Reimagining Church as Event: Perspectives from the Margins
Series Editors: George Zachariah and Sudipta Singh

In these eleven volumes, a collective of Indian theologians envisions Church as an Event that happens in particular contexts in the life of the communities at the margins. They argue that in the life of the communities who experience on their bodies the violence and hegemony of dominant power relations, morality, and religious dogmas and practices, the church happens as countercultural experiences that disrupt the logic of the prevailing order. These experiences enable and empower them to affirm and celebrate their differences, knowledges and beauty even as they weave their liberation. Church as event is a call to rising to life, creating life-flourishing communities that live out the foretaste of the reign of God.

Titles in this Series

Church and Religious Diversity Joshua Samuel and Samuel Mall
Church and Gender Justice Aruna Gnanadason
Faith in the Age of Empire Y.T. Vinayaraj
Dalitekklesia: A Church from Below Raj Bharat Patta
Church and Climate Justice Vinod Wesley
Church and Disability Samuel George
Church and Diakonia in the Age of COVID-19 Mothy Varkey
Decolonising Oikoumene Gladson Jathanna
Church and Human Sexuality Arvind Theodore
With Many Voices: Liturgies in Context Viji Varghese Eapen (Ed.)
The Word becoming Flesh George Zachariah

The Word *becoming* Flesh

George Zachariah

2020

The Word *becoming* **Flesh**- jointly published by the Indian Society for Promoting Christian Knowledge (ISPCK), Post Box 1585, Kashmere Gate, Delhi-110006 and Council for World Mission, Singapore-338729.

Online order: http://ispck.org.in/book.php

Also available on amazon.in

ISBN: 978-93-88945-78-3

Kindle Edition: 978-93-88945-90-5

Cover Picture Credit : Immanuel Paul Vivekanandh K

Laser typeset by

ISPCK, Post Box 1585, 1654, Madarsa Road, Kashmere Gate, Delhi-110006 • *Tel:* 23866323

e-mail: ashish@ispck.org.in • ella@ispck.org.in
website: www.ispck.org.in

*This book was made possible through
the kind contribution of the Council for World Mission*

Dedicated
to the Communities of
the Gurukul Lutheran Theological College
and Research Institute, Chennai
and
the United Theological College, Bengaluru

Speak, this brief time is ample
Before the dying of the body and tongue
Speak, for truth still lives,
Speak, to say what needs to be said

Faiz Ahmed Faiz

For if you keep silence at such a time as this…

Esther 4:14

Contents

Foreword

DISCERNMENT AND RADICAL ENGAGEMENT (DARE) is an initiative of the Council for World Mission (CWM) to enable faith communities to *clarify what it means to engage in* public witness to God's justice and peace in a corrupt and conflicted world.

> The mission of DARE is conceived as the coming together of (a) the *radical soul* of discernment and sense-making in theology and biblical criticism; (b) the yearnings for *signifying engagement* that rise out of the slums of modernism and the valleys of despair; and (c) the commitment to redemption songs that *inspire disturbance* at the hubs of power.

As part of the DARE initiative, each region of CWM is invited to prepare and share biblical and theological resources on current themes and issues being considered by CWM, drawing upon the experiences and resources from the region.

Interfaith Engagement, Ecumenism and Inclusive communities against dehumanising social categorisations are the themes for the book series undertaken by the South Asia region of CWM. The thrust is centred on **Reimagining Church as Event: Perspectives from the Margins**. It calls to the fore persons living in the margins and highlights their voice, their narratives and their passion for a rearrangement of life in communities, as we know it, and a commitment to rise to life and to break out from Babylon. These books are intended for the use of lay people, pastors and evangelists as well as for theological students and seminaries. The series offer stories and narratives, analyses, liturgical resources, biblical, theological and ethical reflections, and missional/praxis proposals.

Church is an event that happens at the margins of contemporary life. Church happens as an epiphanic event where the divine presence is manifested and experienced in the pathos, struggles, contestations and harmonies of everyday existence. Church happens in those spaces where we celebrate the presence of Jesus, the Christ, in the flourishing of life. Church happens when we are transformed by one another, and inspired and enabled to engage in the transformative politics of the reign of God. Church happens whenever and wherever spirit-filled communities reclaim their subversive moral agency and contest the logic and practices of domination and exclusion. Church happens when the community experiences the healing power of the wounded healer and join Jesus in this risk-taking mission, despite the wounds we bear. To reimagine Church requires courage and commitment to engage in the mission of nurturing and organising communities of resistance and healing. This book series is a humble attempt at exposing and encouraging this radical expression of Church.

I appreciate and thank all those who are associated with this series, the authors, the contributors, the publishers and the editors. I commend this book series in the hope and prayers that they will help the faith communities in South Asia, and beyond, to *discern God's presence in community and dare to engage* in ways that re-present the God of life in communities and in the public square, *Rising to Life: Living out the New Heaven and New Earth.*

Colin Cowan
General Secretary
Council for World Mission

Introduction

*Monica Jyotsna Melanchthon**

---

*What does the Lord require of you? To do justice, and to love kindness,
and to walk humbly with your God.*[1]

*May every individual Christian be clear that so long as his (sic!) faith
is in a snail's shell, …he (sic) has not yet come to believe!*[2]

To introduce a set of reflections/essays that one has not written or selected is to perhaps risk misreading the intention of the author. I draw my legitimacy for agreeing to this task from the simple fact that I am trained as a biblical scholar who has interests in context, and commitments to the marginalised in culture, economics, politics, religion and gender. My interpretation of the biblical text takes place against and within a social-cultural, political theological framework. The engagement of the Bible in conversation with contemporary issues and native texts stimulates my work. I have benefitted from and been challenged by George Zachariah's reflections and presentations over the many years that I have known him. Anyone familiar with his work would be able to recognise that these reflections bring together issues and concerns close to and related to Zachariah's expertise in the field of ethics, his research interests, his commitment to transformation of the church and society, his engagement with social activists, his faith and his ongoing involvement in the life of the church.

The Transforming Potential of the Bible

The Bible plays a significant role in the life of an Indian churchgoer. It is the primary, though not exclusive, medium of the community's understanding of God's being and acts. It is mostly read with the expectation of answers to problems in an individual's life. But the human economy as experienced today is skewed, damaged, and tilted in favour of a few and against the earth. The Bible provides a robust framework to address questions of social injustice, human oppression, power, greed and human indignity, and a moral ecology in terms of how God wants us to live with each other and with the earth. Unfortunately, there is insufficient cultural consensus regarding not only the nature of the Bible and how its authority is to be understood but how it is to be read and interpreted. The Indian reader of the Bible has been to a large extent shielded from the scholarly debates that characterise formal biblical studies but, more importantly and sadly, sheltered from the insights offered by the many new and modern and contextual methods of interpretation that are liberational, transformative and justice-oriented. The Bible has been domesticated, its power and potential to establish a basis for social change and justice diminished. It is therefore helpful to be reminded that,

> The interpretation of Scripture begins in the life experience of listening in faith as the Word of God is read and taught and of obedient conduct guided by this Word. Among the truths experienced in this way, the biblical message of justice creates a basic loyalty to the poor and weak and a commitment to their defense. Scripture is then interpreted in the light of this biblically formed understanding.[3]

Bible and Social Ethics

What this collection does is to set before us Zachariah's musings, reflections and insights derived from a conversation/dialogue between the scriptural witness, social ethics, and the many social ills that ail contemporary India. Zachariah brings to life Karl Barth's caution and well-known advice about evaluating world events—"with Bible in one hand and Newspaper in the other,"—that one should seek to assess current events in the light of the Bible.

James Gustafson reminds us that "Biblical social ethics can be a complex task since the ethicist needs competency in biblical studies and the biblical studies scholar needs to have sophistication in ethical thought."[4] Articulating biblical social ethics requires a double consciousness/competency—recognising the value of scripture and interpreting its ethical meaning for us today. Zachariah stands amidst many recent scholars with a vision for contemporary social transformation, who have drawn upon the biblical yearning and dictates for action. He brings his own skill and experience, the knowledge and insight shared by social thinkers/analysts and interpretations offered by biblical scholars to bear upon his reflections. These essays therefore reflect an approach that is interdisciplinary for they are an attempt to bring biblical insight and ethical thought into dialogue and to derive strategies for social change, transformation of society and the church, and establishment of justice in contemporary India. They are a sincere grappling with questions and convictions that are genuine and honest and urgent. They expose a serious engagement and wrestling with key and pertinent issues such as ecology, poverty, sexism, caste, development, what it means to be church, faith, and discipleship. By engaging the biblical text, they lead us deeper and ground us in the cherished heritage of scripture and its theological rigour and visions for a transformed society. But they also steer us towards a just and transformed future, which a rootedness in God's Word would reveal, if only we would actively read it, hear it, be disturbed by it, be motivated by it and embody it.

Word Becoming Flesh

Zachariah has chosen the well-known phrase "Word becoming flesh" as the title for these reflections, deriving inspiration from John 1:14. Indian theologians, particularly Dalit theologians, have emphasised this aspect of God who does not only become flesh but also chooses to dwell among us[5]. Jesus as the 'Word of God' is Immanuel—God with us, but more importantly a God who descends and a God who enters and steps into the context of humanity,[6]—a humanity that is often resistant to God's presence, expectations and desires. Yet this God persists and perseveres and insists on being involved and does not give up on this rebellious humanity. God is in the thick of everything we are going through, a belief that we need to hold on to in the midst of the crisis we are currently in. God is present in this messiness that characterises life today.

African American theologian Shawn Copeland says:

> God is more in our messiness than in what we construct as beautiful…our rituals and sacrifices are not going to bring God around to our causes. What God is looking for from us is mercy and love toward the children, women and men made least among us. What God is looking for is active commitment to justice for those we have dispossessed.[7]

God loves the world and has entered it to save it (John 3:16–17). This God is therefore immediate and direct, bound up with life's material and physical realities and needs. Our political and social engagement with the world concretises the immanence of this God.

As human beings we are created in the image and the likeness of God. We reflect the God who created us. This notion is not always at the forefront of our thinking or our acting. We need to effectively reflect the image and likeness of God inherent in each of us by emulating our God, this God's ways, and this God's holiness.[8] God's holiness defines not only God's being but also God's relationship with the world and humanity (You shall be holy, for I the Lord am holy ~ Lev 19:2).

> The holiness demanded here is ethical and not just ritual…. It therefore follows that God's laws are themselves an expression of his (*sic*) God's being and that is why any sin is considered an attack on God (Psalm 51:6).[9]

Our theology and our missional engagement needs to arise out of commitment to a holy, living, loving and just God, an ethical divinity who protects and defends the cause of the poor, the suffering, the discriminated; who fills the hungry with food and sends the rich away empty (Luke 4). Our belief in and our relationship with this God is realised in tangible ways when we express our love for our brothers and sisters, especially those that have been oppressed and are suffering. These essays therefore remind us that our theological interpretations, our mission strategies, our evaluation of the cultures we belong to and the social and ecclesial structures we establish and adhere to must concur with the preferences of the God we acknowledge and the values of the Christian Gospel.

Discipleship: Enfleshing Love and Justice

A practical biblical and ethical perspective on the church's ministry to the marginalised, the disenfranchised, the discriminated and the oppressed could perhaps take inspiration from this Gospel from which is derived the title of this collection of essays. The Gospel of John contains rich and strong affirmations of the person, work and crucifixion of Jesus Christ, God manifest, whose humanity is also tied with our very own humanity. Jesus responds immediately to issues of brokenness and displacement, of pain and struggle, underlining them as marks of Christian living. Sensitivity, empathy, compassion, accompaniment, inclusivity, love, which sometimes came across as rebellion, resistance, confrontation, countering, crossing borders, troublemaking, struggle are the recorded acts of his ministry and these actually model the call of the church. Embedded in these passions/acts/attitudes is, I believe, a thirst and a commitment to justice and fairness, all of which cannot be imparted as theological constructs. These are learned behaviours, inculcated within the home where we are taught to be observant and vigilant to another[10], which can then move to wider concern for others and the earth.

This is evident, for example, in Jesus' command to the disciple called John, also called 'the beloved', whose witness and mission reveal aspects of discipleship. Mary had just witnessed the brutal and brazen killing of her son. Jesus calls out to both his mother and to John from the cross, with the words, "Woman, here is your son." Then he said to the disciple, "Here is your Mother." As said above, the grounding for Christian living begins within the home where we are called/trained and required to be attentive to one another—to a child, a parent, a brother, or a sister. This preparation within the home prepares you for extending the same principles of concern to the larger society. It has therefore been suggested that John's vocation as disciple was launched by these words of Jesus on the cross. John responds to that call/

request by Jesus Christ to demonstrate that love that John had witnessed in many of Jesus' actions, in the immediate context of the pain and anguish of Mary (John 19: 26-27).[11] The disciple then took Mary into his own home. In reaching out to Mary, John provides us with a glimpse of holistic witness to the love and commitments of the crucified Christ. This initiation of his ministry through a significant act of love, compassion and accompaniment to a grieving mother is only the starting point. But these are not to be seen as options within the framework of Christian discipleship. In other words, we really do not have a choice if we see ourselves as "lovers of Christ." They are obligatory since they flow from the same heart of the one whom we have accepted as Lord and Saviour and who launches each of us and the church into a calling and vocation as followers, as disciples, or as ministers or Word and Sacrament. Discipleship is being a prophetic presence and embodying the call to social justice and holiness that is characteristic of Jesus' work and the Hebrew prophets. We engage in true discipleship understood also as a call to incarnate the compassion and activism of Jesus and the biblical witness in concrete terms for the sake of the poor and the marginalised. To embrace this form of discipleship means that we will always be in creative tension with the powers that be and the systems and structures of governance and control. The broken and painful world, the resistant and fractured world, the divided and suffering world, we are in, is the "locus of political discipleship." [12]

Chapters

In the following pages we shall see that the heart of biblical thought, as presented by Zachariah, mandates efforts to correct economic and social injustices in our communities. Scripture analysed and interpreted with the knowledge of the social sciences and ethical categories of justice, compassion, fairness, solidarity help us understand not only Scripture but also the social world in which we live. By bringing the current context to bear upon the biblical text, new questions arise, and new, and instructive insights are derived for the well-being and transformation of the church.

The fist essay is a postcolonial reading of the story of the magi and their journey to Bethlehem in the Gospel of Matthew, to visit Jesus read through the lens of the victims of the Bhopal tragedy. Zachariah highlights the importance of discerning the signs of the times. He writes, "Discernment of the signs of the times is the starting point of our commitment to become missional communities in the midst of empire. The signs of the times will midwife the birth of a church in the margins."

In what follows, Zachariah identifies these signs and what our responses might be with the help of Scripture.

- In chapter Two he attends to the issue of the domestication of God and the inability of the church to hear God's voice through a reading of 1 Sam 2.

- Chapter Three is a postcolonial reading of the demoniac in Luke 8: 26-39 and the need for boundary crossing, to drive out "the imperial presence in the land." Jesus' exorcism of the demoniac, Zachariah claims, frees the land and its people from the occupying powers and gives it back to the people.

- Chapter Four, reflects on the story of Mary and Martha as found in Luke 10: 38-42 and highlights the problem of sexism and stereotyped "images of the ideal Christian woman." Using the hermeneutics of suspicion and remembrance, Zachariah questions the patriarchy embedded within the text which seeks to polarise women and pits "the apostolic women of the Jesus movement against each other and uses Jesus' words to restrict women's ministry and authority."

- In the fifth chapter, Zachariah, using a postcolonial Dalit feminist lens, calls attention to oft-neglected characters, the group of 'prostituted women,' referred to in the parable of the prodigal son. By giving voice to these silent characters, Zachariah breathes life into them, thereby enabling them to utter their cry of helplessness. Deriving insight from stories of prostituted women today, Zachariah provocatively asks, "Is there a 'Father' who is deeply concerned about the systems that make women prostitutes, and committed to the redemption of those systems and its victims?"

- The sixth chapter attends to Genesis 1: 1-2 to respond to ecological concerns confronting the world today and affirms the fact that we are to join the Holy Spirit that empowers us for the work of transformation.

- Chapter Seven continues addressing the theme of ecology and uses the well-known creation Hymn Psalm 104 to emphasise the mutual dependence of the created order and our call to partner with God to renew the face of the earth.

- Romans 8: 8-17 is the focus in chapter Eight, addressing once again the groaning of creation because of "deep-rooted sin and injustice in the social fabric." The sound of earth's groaning is the cry of the earth against structural sin and injustice. But the groaning of the earth is also the cry of the earth in labour as it brings forth 'new epiphanies' and 'an alternative imagination of God', of alternative visions that are hope giving.

- Chapter Nine visits Revelation 21:6 and 22:17 to highlight the water crisis, the pollution of our waterbodies, the lack of water experienced by the slum dwelling poor and the competition for it between moneyed and imperial corporations. The absence of the sea in this biblical text is 'hope giving' according to Zachariah since it means the destruction of a greedy imperial political economy that controls and exploits the waterbodies at the expense of the poor. Rev 21:6 promises water as a free gift for all and a healing, a redeemed earth that is the outcome of divine activity in partnership with the entire creation.

- What is the significance of children in messianic politics and Christian discipleship? Chapter Ten considers the child in Mark 9: 30-37 who stands "as the epitome of all victims, victimised by dominating power relations, exclusion, hegemony, and systematic silencing. The constructive dimension of Jesus' messianic politics attempts here to create alternative social relations by bringing the marginalised into the centre and giving voice to the silenced ones."

- Chapter Eleven analyses John 20: 24-29 by bringing it into conversation with the tale of King Maveli and the festival of Onam. This juxtaposed reading questions atonement theology, the popular understanding, and interpretations of the meaning of resurrection and the wounded Christ. Zachariah concludes, "It is an invitation to follow the wounded God into the open wounds in our midst. It is in the open wounds of our times that we meet the Risen Lord."

- What does the parable of the wicked tenants in Matthew 21: 33-46 have to do with the Reformation? Chapter Twelve draws insights from the parable to invite the church into a time of introspection and repentance.

- Drawing on Mark 12: 41-44 and the meagre offerings of the poor widow, and the temple system in ancient Israel, chapter Thirteen calls for the church to be open to always being reformed.

- In chapter Fourteen, Zachariah reflects on the meaning of Lent and counters a Lenten "spirituality that rejects materiality." Using varied texts from both the Old and the New Testaments he offers alternative understandings of Lent that call for engagement with the community.

- Chapter Fifteen's focus on the resurrection story in Mark 16: 1-20 is an invitation for the church to live its life as an Easter community, to be one that rolls the stone away from all that denies hope and life.

- Chapter Sixteen, entitled "Faith in the context of God forsakenness," engages with the words of the Prophet Habakkuk in 1: 1-4 and 2: 1-4. When our faith, Zachariah maintains, "is formulated in the everyday living experiences of the wretched of the earth, we develop the revolutionary patience to wait for the realisation of that new heaven and new earth."

- Chapter Seventeen visits Exodus 32 to point us towards the need to dismantle false gods/ungods of caste privilege, wealth, power, and the like, towards the worship of the true God.

- Chapter Eighteen reflects Acts 5: 27-42 and the Pentecost and the tensions that exist between civil/temporal authorities and Christian discipleship and how we might address this tension.

- In Chapter Nineteen, Zachariah reads Romans 12:2 as a call to Christian discipleship that requires non-conformism, the courage to sin boldly and a commitment to creative maladjustment, all for the sake of life.

- Chapter Twenty reconsiders the 'Magnificat,' and the figure of Mary and her reasons for agreeing to become the mother—one of which was her belief in "the politics of the system-threatening reign of God."

- The last reflection is entitled "Called to be Troublemakers." With a focus on 1 Kings 18:17 and Matthew 10: 34-39, the essay calls attention to the life and work of Oscar Romero, of El Salvador, who upon seeing the suffering of the people went against the expectations of the church and interpreted his calling as that of creating breaches— breaches that expose the sin of the church and those in positions of power, of sinful systems, both political and ecclesial. Zachariah encourages the church to don on the mantle of Elijah the prophet and be recognised as a "troublemaker."

Reading, studying and interpreting the Bible is a matter of faith. Biblical research and study are not merely an academic/ intellectual exercise but ultimately a way to respond to God. These reflections apply Scripture to the problems of society and are directed to the membership of the church. The aim is to stir the imagination of the reader and to provoke action. We as the church have the authority and the wherewithal to achieve justice and transform social structures if we have the will to become a counter-community that shakes, confronts and destabilises the status quo and its bias in favour of the dominant. It is hoped that these essays seen both as a synthesis of biblical studies and ethics and as a series of reflections on what it means to witness to the imperatives of the Gospel of Jesus Christ in a fractured and groaning world contribute to enfleshing the Word towards transformation and change.

Endnotes

* **The Rev. Dr. Monica Jyotsna Melanchthon** is a church worker (ordained by the Andhra Evangelical Lutheran Church, India) and theological educator. She currently teaches Hebrew Bible/Old Testament at the *Pilgrim Theological College, University of Divinity* (Melbourne, Australia) and has published in various academic books focusing on interpretations of Old Testament texts from the Indian context and the perspectives of the marginalized. Her current projects include a feminist commentary on 1 Kings for the Wisdom Commentary Series (Liturgical Press) and an Earth Bible Commentary on Joshua 1–11 (Bloomsbury).

[1] Micah 6:8.

[2] Karl Barth, *Dogmatics in Outline,* trans. G. T. Thompson (London: SCM Press,1949), 33.

[3] Stephen Charles Mott, *Biblical Ethics and Social Change.* 2nd ed. (Oxford/ NY: Oxford University Press, 2011), xii.

[4] James M. Gustafson, "The Place of Scripture in Christian Ethics: A Methodological Study," *Interpretation* 24 (1970): 430.

[5] V Devasahayam, *Outside the Camp: Bible Studies in Dalit Perspective* (Chennai: Gurukul, 1992).

[6] ZA Blog, "What does it mean that the Word became flesh?" https:// zondervanacademic.com/blog/word-became-flesh (March 26, 2018).

[7] Shawn Copeland in an interview, in *Enfleshing Theology: Embodiment, Discipleship and Politics in the Work of M Shawn Copeland,* Robert J Rivera and Michele Saracino (eds.), (New York: Lexington Books/Fortress Academic, 2018). https://www.amazon.com.au/dp/1978704054/ref=rdr_kindle_ext_ tmb#reader_B07HR2ZYH3.

[8] Allowing the abuse of another human being suggests that we are not only blind to the Divine but also abuse the Divine present within that human being (Oscar Romero).

[9] Victor Zinkuratire, "Isaiah 1-39," in Daniel Patte (ed), *The Global Bible Commentary* (Nashville: Abingdon, 2004):186.

[10] Shawn Copeland in an interview, in *Enfleshing Theology: Embodiment, Discipleship and Politics in the Work of M Shawn Copeland*

[11] Harold Dean Trulear, "Go and Do Likewise: The Church's Role in Caring for Crime Victims," in Lisa Barnes Lampman (ed.), and Michelle D Shattuck (Assoc Ed.), *God and the Victim: Theological Reflections on Evil, Victimization, Justice and Forgiveness* (Grand Rapids, MI: Eerdmans, 1999), 71.

[12] Shawn Copeland in an interview, in *Enfleshing Theology: Embodiment, Discipleship and Politics in the Work of M Shawn Copeland.*

Prologue

Bible is a resource that can inspire, convict, condemn, transform and heal us and our communities. Reading the Bible from locations of power and privilege makes the Bible a hegemonic weapon to perpetuate the prevailing order built on the shoulders of the subalterns. The subaltern imagination to reclaim the Word and to read their stories in the Scripture has transformed biblical texts into a counter-hegemonic resource for liberation. For those of us who continue to cherish and benefit from our caste, gender and class privilege, wrestling with the Bible, informed by the voices from the margins, can become a "Damascus experience," unmasking our privilege and hypocrisy.

The Word becoming Flesh is a compilation of biblical reflections and homilies spoken, written, and published over a period of ten years in my own discipleship journey. They reflect the angst, ambiguities, fear, doubts, frustrations and hope of a person engaged in the ministry of theological education. These words were originally addressed to seminary communities, inviting us to become self-reflexive so that we can develop alternative imaginations and convictions about our call and witness. In this journey, I was inspired, challenged and nourished by the love and solidarity of the communities of the Gurukul

Lutheran Theological College and Research Institute, Chennai, and the United Theological College, Bengaluru. I acknowledge the warmth and support of my friends Samuel Abraham, Sunil Caleb, Monica Jyotsna Melanchthon and Sudipta Singh who accompanied me on this journey. I hope and pray that these reflections will inspire us to enflesh our faith even as we witness the Word becoming flesh in our midst.

1

Anamnestic Solidarity
Matthew 2: 1-18

It was a winter night in December 1984. The city of Bhopal lay frozen with a cold wind blowing. Sometime during the night that cold wind turned into the angel of death. The wind carried the poisonous gas that leaked from the Union Carbide plant in the city. It was India's Hiroshima. For thousands, it was their last night. Those who survived the gas tragedy became the living dead. Yet another casualty was the environment. The lifeworld could literally smell the colonisation of its being, while the state and the multinational corporation legitimised the 'genocide' as a sacrifice that the subjects of an "underdeveloped" nation were called to bear for the sake of progress and growth.

Union Carbide, the American multinational corporation, built the Bhopal plant in 1979 to manufacture methyl isocyanate, an extremely hazardous compound used to make Sevin, a pesticide used in cotton, corn and vegetable farming. Union Carbide declared that the plant was the realisation of the corporation's "dream of lighting a new star in the Indian sky." Protests against establishing the plant in the densely populated city fell on deaf ears. The American capitalists insisted that the factory should be set up in the city because it was more expensive to set one up in a less-populated area. Safety systems fell below the standards observed in the company's plants in the United States; they were given a go-by to maximise profit. An internal audit conducted by staff from the Virginia plant of the company, three months before the explosion, had warned of the possibility of a disaster waiting to happen. But the company ignored it. In September 1982, journalist Rajkumar Keswani published a series of articles based on his examination of the company and the plant, saying: "Bhopal: we are sitting on a volcano…. The day is not far off when Bhopal will be a dead city, when only scattered stones and debris will bear witness to its tragic end."[1] But a minister in the state of Madhya Pradesh responded: "There is no cause for concern about the presence of the Carbide factory because the phosgene it produces is not a toxic gas."[2] The rest is history.

Even after three decades, Union Carbide is reluctant to reveal the nature of the chemical releases or their toxicity, making the medical treatment of the survivors difficult. According to conservative statistics, at least 100,000 people sustained injuries and disability from gas inhalation, including birth defects and disease of lungs and eyes. Three thousand seven hundred people lost their lives.

Union Carbide finally negotiated a settlement of $470 million—$800 per plaintiff—but spent more than $100 million on legal fees and public relations. The victims were betrayed by the corporation and the Indian government. They were not consulted about the settlement, and no child under the age of 18 could file a claim.

In 1962, when Rachel Carson in her book *Silent Spring* asked the question, "Can anyone believe it is possible to lay down such a barrage of poison on the surface of the earth without making it unfit for all life?"[3] *Time* magazine ridiculed her, calling it "an emotional and inaccurate outburst." But within two decades, her forthtelling became a reality in Bhopal: "It was a spring without voices. On the mornings that had once throbbed with the dawn chorus of robins, catbirds, doves, hays, wrens and scores of other bird voices, there was no sound. Only silence lay over the fields and woods and marsh."[4]

Bhopal was not an accident; it was collateral damage in the civilising mission of transnational capital. These people were considered 'disposable' and their lifeworld were sacrificed at the altar of development and progress to make their nation proud.

The laments emerging from Bhopal echo the weeping of the mothers of Ramah and Bethlehem. As empire continues to strike, we hear similar cries from different parts of the world. What is the theological significance of the memories of tortured bodies? How do we engage with the memories of lives offered as sacrifice to consolidate and perpetuate imperial aggression and corporate greed? Dangerous memories, according to Johann Baptist Metz, are "memories which make demands on us. These are memories in which earlier experiences break through to the center-point of our lives and reveal new and dangerous insights for the present."[5] Dangerous memories are subversive memories. Our remembrance of the victims of Bhopal and all other victims of imperial plunder is a political and spiritual praxis, inviting and inspiring us to witness to God in the midst of the "impossibility of life" through ministries of protest, resistance and alternatives.

"Anamnestic solidarity," as Mark Lewis Taylor puts it, is profoundly theological, "as remembrance of the dead constitutes an effect of the dead in the present that re-members, re-constitutes, living communities."[6] In other words, our solidarity with the dead and the tortured affirms that they are co-present in our contemporary struggles against different manifestations of empire. Their co-presence strengthens and empowers those who continue to experience death in our times, and fight against it.

Sister Diana Ortiz, an American Catholic missionary in Guatemala who was tortured by the state and incarcerated for years, reflects on this experience of anamnestic solidarity in her autobiographical book, *The Blindfold's Eyes: My Story from Torture to Truth*: "We believe the spirits of our tortured sisters and brothers who have gone before us dwell within us, giving us the strength to hold firm to our convictions of justice for all people and to bear witness to the heinous atrocities committed by oppressive governments."[7] We see this spirit in the observance of the anniversary of the Bhopal massacre, where communities that dream about life in the midst of the impossibility of life gather strength from the dangerous memories of the slain to create a world devoid of empire.

The story of the murder of innocent children narrated by Matthew in his infancy narrative enables us to celebrate the dangerous memory of the martyred children even as we confront similar experiences of brutal torture and murder by imperial powers. The Roman Catholic Church observes December 28 as the Feast of the Holy Innocents, and the collect for the day is an inspiring and challenging one:

> We remember today, O God, the slaughter of the holy innocents of Bethlehem by King Herod. Receive, we pray, into the arms of your mercy all innocent victims; and by your great might frustrate the designs of evil tyrants and establish your rule of justice, love, and peace; through Jesus Christ our Lord, who lives

and reigns with you, in the unity of the Holy Spirit, one God, forever and ever. Amen.[8]

It is a strange coincidence that both the Bhopal story and the Matthean narrative begin with the metaphor of a 'star'. Union Carbide announced its entry into "underdeveloped" India with the promise that the plant would be a star on the Indian sky to lead the country to greater heights in industrial and economic development. Warren Carter in his commentary of Matthew observes that there were stories that associated stars with the birth of significant figures. The magi were

> observant enough to notice it, motivated enough to travel some distance to identify the special person to whom the star bears witness, astute enough to know that the star attest a new king, and discerning enough to know that worship is the appropriate response.[9]

Stars hence signify the beginning of a new eon—a new order where the legitimacy of the prevailing order is contested, and alternatives experimented.

Bhopal is the living example of subaltern communities whose environment is colonised and destroyed in the name of development and progress. The star that the American corporation lit on the Indian sky was the inauguration of an unholy alliance between transnational capital, modern science and technology, national elites, and the postcolonial state. The coexistence of massacre and accumulation is the hallmark of dominant scientific and technological projects. The nexus between technology and capital motivated by profit led to the Bhopal gas tragedy where the victims were subjected to a scientific gaze but are yet to be justly healed and compensated. The Indian Council of Medical Research is even reluctant to respect the demands of the victims to have access to the scientific researches, conducted by it, on the effects of the gas leak. This is not only an issue of information about the treatment of their poison-ravaged bodies but also their right to have access to scientific research to know the health condition of their children. After three decades, reports of groundwater quality from Madhya Pradesh Pollution Control Board reveals that "chemicals that can cause damage to brain, lungs, liver, and kidneys and give rise to cancers and birth defects are present in high concentrations in the water of the local community hand pumps."[10] The star that Union Carbide lit on the Indian sky marked the beginning of the 'corporatisation' and 'commodification' of the commons and subsistence communities in order to facilitate corporate plunder.

The story of the magi also starts with the appearance of a star in the sky. The magi were equipped as well as committed to recognising and identifying non-conventional occurrences in their surroundings. That is how they observed a special star in the sky which stood different from the rest of the stars. They discerned the star as a sign of *kairos*, which demanded a response from them. So, they decided to reflect upon this sign. They got into the world of research to interpret the sign and concluded that the star proclaimed the birth of a new king. They decided to embark on a journey to meet this new king and pay homage to him. But they were unsure of how to locate and identify this newborn king. Finally, they decided to follow the dominant and conventional wisdom. By time-honoured logic, a king could be born in Jerusalem in the palace of Herod. So, they started their journey to the palace.

The story started with the audacity of the magi to believe in the possibility of the birth of a new king when Herod was in power. However, as Matthew narrates, the discernment of alternatives was incorporated into the dominant logic of searching for alternatives in palaces. Imperial co-option of alternatives is not a recent phenomenon. Co-option of people's commitment to search for alternatives disables the moral agency of the community to envision dreams and strive for their realisation outside the logic of the prevailing order. The temptation to assume the centre as the locus of alternatives, which is the dominant pattern, is common in our times. We are all mesmerised by the lure of empire that we have sold our souls to it. Even alternatives have become NGO projects funded by corporate houses!

A critical analysis of the discernment of the magi and the path they followed in their search for the newborn king provide us theological insights that are relevant today. Discernment of mission in the midst of empire does not start from doctrines or scriptures or sacraments; rather, it begins with our engagement with the signs of the times. It is not the sources of faith that should lead us to the context. Rather the signs of the times provide us new hermeneutical tools to engage with the sources of our faith. When we read the Scripture and tradition and celebrate the sacraments, informed by the signs of the times, these sources of faith become catalysts, inspiring us to transform our contexts. The magi started their journey by identifying the star as the sign of the times and interpreting it as the symbol of the birth of a new king. But once they set out on the journey, they ignored the sign and followed the dominant route and ended up in the palace of King Herod.

The encounter with King Herod was a tutorial for the magi. It opened their eyes to the inherent contradictions in all imperial powers. Herod, the King of the Jews, was frightened at the birth of a child who was the symbol of marginality and vulnerability.

Realising their mistake, the magi started their journey again, following the star.

A journey following the star—the sign of the times—will always lead us to the margins. The margin is the place where people who bear the weight of the world are destined to live. Our journey to the margins offers us a different experience of epiphany. Such journeys provide us with visions that unsettle the prevailing order. So, margins are the revelatory sites of exposure and disclosure. The signs of the times take us to the manger from the centres of imperial power. The manger is not a symbol of humility or simplicity, which God has chosen as the location for God's meek and mild child to be born. The manger symbolises rejection, exclusion and negation. The manger is symbolic of God's identification with all who are denied their basic human rights to live a dignified life because of their economic status, caste, race, gender and sexual orientation. The star stopped at the place where the baby was. The signs of the times always act as a window to the margins, inviting us to meet God in the company of the wretched of the earth. The magi saw the child surrounded with farm animals and shepherds—symbols of subalternity, pollution and dirt.

Our reluctance to follow the signs of the times as guiding perspectives in our mission engagement is often thought of as a naive omission or an innocent mistake. That is not true. We are so indoctrinated by the dominant trajectories of mission and theology that even without our knowledge we follow the dominant perspective which is convenient and comfortable to all of us. Since it is status quoist, it does not involve any risk. Doing mission around Jerusalem is rewarding because of the proximity to political, economic and religious power centres. But the story of the magi reminds us of the consequences of our mission at the centres of power. Dominant trajectories of mission have consequences. Such mission begets death and destruction. For the magi, their reluctance to follow the star was just an innocent mistake. But it led to the slaughter of hundreds of innocent children.

Discernment of the signs of the times is the starting point of our commitment to become missional communities in the midst of empire. The signs of the times will midwife the birth of a church in the margins. We live in a context where empire continues to colonise our minds, bodies, seeds, worldviews, lands, waters and forests. The mission paradigms that offer us prosperity, privilege and bright futures lure us to search for God in the palace. We have lost our ability to see and hear the laments of Rachels in our times. When the community of the wise people followed the signs of the times, they were able to experience God in the manger. That was an experience of *metanoia*. They became a transformed community and took another road to return to their place. What we see here is the happening of a transformed missional community. Empowered by the epiphany experience of God in the vulnerable child, and inspired by the communities in the margins, the magi decided to come out of empire. The different route here signifies a route different from the road to empire. This is the challenge that we need to undertake even as we strive to transform our communities in the midst of empire.

What is the theological significance of the massacre of the innocent children in the Matthean infancy narrative? What is the message of hope that Mary's child offers to the mothers of Bethlehem, Auschwitz, Gaza, Kashmir, Delhi and Bhopal who refuse to be consoled? How do we celebrate Christmas even as we continue to experience the impossibility of life? As Nancy Rockwell rightly observes,

> The story tells us that our salvation is born in the midst of such times, into the heart of our darkness, in a moment when time is shattered, and new time begins. And our salvation is brought to us by a survivor of the worst that can befall, by a child whose light was not extinguished, a child who understands deeply what has happened, a child who remembers, a child who was not killed.[11]

With this new realisation of the divine, mothers who refuse to be consoled are engaged in creating a new world where death is overcome by the beauty of life. "Devastated by the slaughter, picking up their splintered lives, their broken hearts, their stabbing fears, their traumatized surviving children, they also found among the wreckage the words that promise the Messiah will be born to them, especially to them. They carried this promise, in tears, as they buried their dead children."[12]

We see the same spirit of determination in the mothers of Bhopal powerfully echoed in the poem, "Flames, not Flowers," by Terry Allan:

> But in your quest for profit we refuse to take part. Against all odds we'll live our lives with joy and heart. We believe in the power of the human spirit. We raise our voices together so everyone can hear it. We are the women of the world, we are flames, not flowers. We will not wilt before your corporate power. Hand in hand and heart to heart, side by side, we will fight for justice 'til the day we die.[13]

Where is God in Bhopal? What is the hope for Bhopal? How do the dangerous memories of the slain empower us in our battle against empire? We are called to cry aloud in protest, exposing the sinfulness of empire. We are invited to groan in labour pain, celebrating the end of empire. As Nestor O Miguez puts it,

> Cry out, mothers of pain and of hope…. May your cries of terror resound forever, without ceding to the offers of comfort from those who purchase consciences. Do not listen to the sweet words with which those preachers of undignified reconciliation wish to soften you. May you never cease in your determined lament, that unceremonious demand for life, the endless marches around the town squares; may the demand for justice that rises from the bottom of the centuries and remains to this day never be silenced, so that the Empire may never sleep without feeling, even if it covers its ears, that its massacres have not been forgiven.[14]

Remembrance of dangerous memories is a celebration of all who undergo torture and terror. As Johann Baptist Metz reminds us, "every rebellion against suffering is fed by the subversive power of remembered suffering…. The meaning of our history does not depend only on the survivors, the successful and those who make it. Meaning is not a category that is only reserved for the conquerors!"[15] Rather, the meaning of history lies in the remembrance of the victims whose heads have been crushed by empire. Recalling of their dangerous memories "anticipates the future as a future of those who are oppressed, without hope and doomed to fail. It is therefore a dangerous and at the same time liberating memory that questions the present,"[16] and empowers all who are destined to live under regimes of torture and terror to be the midwives of a new utopia of hope in an imperial world. We witness this faith in the words of Rashida Bee, a Bhopal survivor and activist: "We are not expendable. We are not flowers offered at the altar of profit and power. We are dancing flames committed to conquering darkness and to challenging those who threaten the planet and the magic and mystery of life."[17]

Endnotes

[1] Dominique Lapierre and Javier Moro. *It was Five Past Midnight in Bhopal*, (Delhi: Full Circle. 2001), 180

[2] Lapierre and Moro, 2001, 181

[3] Rachel Carson. *Silent Spring:* (Boston: Houghton Mifflin Company Carson, 1962), xv

[4] Carson, 1962, 2

[5] Johann Baptist Metz, *Faith in History and Society: Toward a Practical Fundamental Theology*, (New York: A Crossroad Book, 1980), 109

[6] Mark Lewis Taylor. *The Theological and the Political: On the Weight of the World,* (Minneapolis: Fortress Press 2011), 203

[7] Diana Ortiz. *The Blindfold's Eyes: My Journey from Torture to Truth.* (Maryknoll, NY: Orbis Books, 2007), 191

[8] https://www.growchristians.org/2017/12/28/i-remember-the-feast-of-the-holy-innocents-and-that-hope-is-hard-to-kill/

[9] Carter. 76

[10] *The Hindu,* April 22, 2008

[11] Nancy Rockwell. *The innocents.* http://www.patheos.com/blogs/biteintheapple/the-innocents/

[12] Nancy Rockwell. *The innocents.* http://www.patheos.com/blogs/biteintheapple/the-innocents/

[13] Allan, n.d "Flames not Flowers" www.bhopal.net/old_studentsforbhopal_org/Assets/Poetry.doc.

[14] Nestor O. Miguez. "Herod's Slaughter of Children and Other Atrocities throughout Time," in Mark Roncace and Joseph Weaver (eds.), *Global Perspectives on the Bible*, (Boston: Pearson, 2014), 217

[15] Johann Baptist Metz. *Faith in History and Society: Toward a Practical Fundamental Theology*, (New York: A Crossroad Book, 1980), 110, 114

[16] Metz, 90

[17] Paul Hawken, *Blessed Unrest: How the Largest Movement in the World Came into Being and Why No One Saw it Coming,* (New York: Viking, 2007), 49

2

Audacity of Hope

1 Samuel 3: 1-20

This is a familiar text narrating the story of Samuel's discernment of the divine call and his submission. The books of Samuel narrate the transition that Israel makes from a tribal society to a monarchical society. Eli and his sons Hophni and Phinehas are priests in the sanctuary of the Lord at Shiloh. Eli, old and virtually blind, is a righteous man, but Hophni and Phinehas are scoundrels who take sacrificial meat for themselves and sexually abuse women who minister at the sanctuary door (1 Samuel 2: 12-17, 22). And Eli is unable to restrain his sons.

Hannah, a barren woman facing stigma and contempt, comes to the sanctuary to share before the Lord her tragic story and her hope of getting a child. Samuel enters into the story as God's response to Hannah's prayer. As promised, Hannah brings Samuel to the sanctuary to lend him to the Lord as a minister at the sanctuary. So, Samuel begins his new life at the sanctuary under the patronage and guidance of Eli. One night, Samuel hears his name being called repeatedly. He eventually discerns it as a call from the Lord and submits himself to the call saying, "Speak, for your servant is listening."

The story of Israel is the story of God calling people to carry on the divine mission. Abraham, Moses, Esther, Isaiah, Jeremiah, Amos, are some and the list goes on. But what is the significance of the call of Samuel for us in our context? At the very beginning of this narrative, we read that "the word of the Lord was rare in those days; visions were not widespread" (3:1). What does the author mean by this? Does the author speak about the silence of God and the inability of the people to see visions in a symbolic manner, or does the author describe an objective state of affairs?

Biblical scholars are of the opinion that the silence of God and the absence of visions is an accurate description of the context. It was a period of political anarchy in Israel's history when "every person did what was right in his own eyes" (Judges 21:25). Moreover, the two sons of Eli, the priests at the sanctuary, were "wicked men who had no regard for the Lord." So, it was a context in which a sense of community was destroyed by people who refused to follow the commands and will of God and instead imposed their worldview and dominant interests on others. Further, religion had lost its vocation of being an agent of divine justice in the community and had deteriorated into a corrupt and violent system that not only oppresses and abuses the powerless but also legitimises the prevailing systems of injustice and domination. In such situations God seems to be silent, because we refuse to listen to a gospel that is different from the prevailing wisdom. Visions are absent because we refuse to believe in the beyond of the present. God *was* silent and visions *were* rare. But we are reminded that in such situations even an insignificant person—a little boy born to a woman who faced ignominy for being 'barren'—can make a difference. This is the audacity of hope that the Christian faith proclaims.

Martin Luther King loved to tell the story of his own discernment of the call. He did not want to become a leader of the civil rights movement. He entered the ministry primarily because his father was a pastor and he wanted to do what his father wished for him. In fact, Dr. King wanted to lead a quiet life as a theological educator. One day he would become the President of Morehouse College. But life was to change one night after he came late and tired during the Montgomery bus boycott. The phone rang. An angry voice at the other end said, "We're gonna get you nigger!" Martin Luther King stood in his kitchen, frozen in fear. He wanted to call his dad for comfort and advice. But Daddy King was not there. Then King heard the voice: "Martin, you do what's right. You stand up for justice. You be my drum major for righteousness. I'll be with you." He had heard his name called. He knew what God wanted for him. His life was forever changed, and through his life, the world was changed.

Dr. King's context was not very different from that of Samuel: The word of the Lord was rare in those days; there was no frequent vision. Epiphany is a reminder that we meet God at the most unexpected places and times. Dr. King knew this, and he discerned God's voice and call as commissioning him to midwife a new hope so that the blacks can one day affirm that they are also created in the image of God. This is the audacity of hope that Martin Luther King instilled in the black folks in America. As he categorically affirmed in his "I have a dream" speech, "We are not satisfied, and we will not be satisfied until justice rolls down like waters and righteousness like a mighty stream."[1] This is the audacity of hope that made James Cone,

Cornel West, Barack Hussein Obama, and a host of others, a possibility.

We live in a context where God seems to be silent in the victory marches of empire and where visions are blurred by the glittering campaign that makes us believe that there is no alternative. It is in this context that people like Babasaheb Ambedkar and Martin Luther King become significant for us. We invoke their memories not with an intention to romanticise them or to say that they are people who are perfect and without blemish. Rather, their witness of nonconformism and vision of change has the potential to help us in our discernment process.

When Samuel woke up hearing the call, Eli stumbled out of his bed and said, "Go back to your sleep, you are a wishful dreamer." This has been the response of the church and all other dominant institutions to all dreamers and visionaries. "Go back to sleep Moses, you cannot even speak properly. Go back to sleep, Ambedkar, you are just dreaming. Go back to sleep, Gandhi, you don't know the might of the British Empire. Go back to sleep, Medha Patkar, you are just a woman. Go back to your classrooms, students, you are just students." Audacity of hope has the power to defeat the tranquilising effect of institutionalised spirituality and politics and to believe that "yes, we can."

We believe in the priesthood of all believers, and hence it is important for us to discern our distinctive call. It is also important for us to engage in some honest introspection, evaluate our discernment and our commitment to participate in the divine praxis in history. Maybe it is hard for us to say "Speak, for your servant is listening" because we are not ready for God to come into our comfort zones and disrupt our projects and dreams. In fact, we have domesticated God and manipulated our understanding of Christian responsibility and witness in such a way that we can continue our business as usual and yet claim that we are God's servants involved in Christian ministry. But living in a context in which God is seemingly silent and visions are rare, God calls us to have the audacity of hope. As Malcolm X, the black nationalist leader, categorically affirmed, "The future belongs to those who prepare for it today." It is this audacity of hope that we need to preach and live out through our lives. The audacity of hope enabled Martin Luther King believe that we will be able to carve out of the mountain of despair a stone of hope.

> With this faith we will be able to transform the jangling discords of our nation into a beautiful symphony of brotherhood and sisterhood. With this faith we will be able to work together, to pray together, to struggle together, to go to jail together, to stand up for freedom together, knowing that we will be free one day.

This is the audacity of hope that God demands from us.

Samuel was not willing to turn his back to the divine call and he responded, "Speak, for your servant is listening" (3:10). As a result, "the word of Samuel came to all Israel" (4:1). Discernment of the call is possible only when we refuse to listen to the dominant advice to continue to sleep. When we respond to the still small voice within us, transgressing the logic of the prevailing order, we become new beings with the potential to unleash a new movement of change in our communities. The audacity of hope for our times is to believe that "yes, we can."

Endnotes

[1] https://ourlutherking.com/i-have-a-dream-speech-text/

[2] https://www.collectiveliberation.org/wp-content/uploads/2013/01/POWER_Where_To_From_Here.pdf

[3] https://ourlutherking.com/i-have-a-dream-speech-text/

3

Crossing the Boundaries with Christ

Luke 8: 26-39

Casting out demons was one of the most significant ministries of Jesus. The healing of the demon-possessed man of Gerasenes (Mark 5: 1-17; Luke 8: 26-37), the casting out of the unclean spirit in the synagogue at Capernaum (Mark 1: 21–28 and Luke 4: 31–37), and the Beelzebul passages (Mark 3, Luke 11, Mark 10, 12) are examples of Jesus' ministry towards demoniacs. All these incidents depict the power of Jesus over demons. In the Gospels, demons are perceived as an organised enemy that opposes the activities of the reign of God. That means, exorcisms were not isolated events of compassion for individuals oppressed by malevolent forces but direct confrontations with the dehumanising forces of evil and the demonstration of the transforming power and presence of the reign of God.

Luke 8: 26-39 narrates the healing of the demon-possessed man in Gerasenes. This incident is described in the other two synoptic Gospels as well. In the Lukan narrative, Jesus invites his disciples to join him to go across to the other side of the sea. During this crossing, a storm blows and the boat begins to shake and sink. The disciples, who are fishermen by profession, experience a situation of total strangeness and fear. "Master, we are perishing," they cried. After rebuking the wind, Jesus asks them, "Where is your faith?"

A journey outside of our comfort zones, the familiar, is always a risky business. It is faith that sustains us on such journeys of boundary crossing.

Jesus and his disciples finally arrive in the country of the Gerasenes on the other side of the sea, which is situated opposite Galilee. Gerasenes is one of the federal cities of the Decapolis. From Mark's point of view, this is a Gentile territory that is alien, which apparently threatens the Jewish population west of the sea. During those days, the enmity and separation between Jews and Gentiles were seen as normal and part of the natural order. Hence, in this incident, Jesus makes a conscious attempt to invite the attention of his disciples to the realities on the other side of the sea through a voyage that crosses boundaries.

As soon as Jesus and his disciples reach the land, there appears a man of the city who is possessed by demons. He has not worn clothes for a long time, and he does not live in a house. He lives among tombs and no one can restrain him. The demoniac is presented as a person who suffers from a self-destructive mentality. He falls before Jesus and pleads with him not to torment him. Unlike similar incidents of exorcism, Jesus here attempts to identify the demon. "What is your name?" Jesus asks him. "Legion and we are many," he answers. 'Legion', a Latin term, meant a division of Roman soldiers. Many such legions were based in Syria to control the Eastern front, including Palestine. Many veterans of the Roman army had been settled in those regions as they were given land as payment for their service.

Legion begs Jesus to send them into a large herd of swine, a group of pigs on the hillside. 'Herd' was another military term commonly used for a group of soldiers. Jesus dismisses them into the herd, and they drown in the waters. Once the demon is out, the man expresses his desire to accompany Jesus. But Jesus refuses and asks him to return home and spread the good news. He returns home proclaiming what God has done for him.

Reading this text afresh in the context of the contemporary manifestations of imperial invasion and occupation prompts us to approach it from a postcolonial perspective. This will enable us to locate the contemporary epiphanies of our times. The self-identification of the demons with the occupying Roman army enables us to identify the land and the people under occupation as possessed by evil forces, and hence in need of Jesus' exorcism and healing. Occupation is more than an act of political invasion. It is a hegemonic act of self-alienation whereby the colonised are indoctrinated to internalise the worldview and ethos of the coloniser. To put it differently, imperial occupation erases the distinct identity and subjectivity of the community.

It is in this context that we look at the exorcism of Jesus. The demons came out of the man and entered a herd of pigs which rushed down the steep bank into the sea. As we have already seen, a 'herd' is also a military term for a group of soldiers. Exorcism in the context of empire hence means returning the imperial legions to the sea from where they came. Sea is perceived as the route of the empire. So, by driving out the imperial presence in the land, Jesus' exorcism has freed the land and its people from the occupying powers and given it back to the people. This text invokes the memory of the destruction of the Egyptian forces in the sea which enabled the Israelite community to inherit the Promised Land.

The story of the demoniac depicts the intimate weaving of the personal and social dimensions of domination and possession. It reveals the dialectic between the (dis)possessed physical body and the (dis)possessed social body. It reiterates the anti-imperial bias of Jesus' ministry. As Larry Rasmussen rightly puts it, "epiphanies always take us beyond our present understanding, beyond the truth we presently know and beyond our comfort level. *Epiphaninein* is a flash of insight, a sudden revelation, new—or old—truth made manifest."[1]

Having met Christ in the context of a land and people occupied by the empire, what does this text say to us in our contemporary context of perennial occupations and invasions? How does this new understanding of Christ beyond boundaries inspire us in our Christian witness?

Epiphanies enable us to see the social location of Jesus. As we see in the story of the demoniac, Jesus is present beyond boundaries, where the land and the people are possessed by occupying forces. When the demoniac possession dispossesses the people of their subjectivity and selfhood, Jesus is present there, enabling the community to reclaim their selfhood and their lost humanity.

Boundaries are constructed and maintained to perpetuate and perpetrate the prevailing order. Boundaries prevent the possibility of dreaming visions of a beyond of the present. Boundaries, thus, legitimise the complex and corporate manifestations of sin in our social body. The epiphanies of Jesus become a counter-narrative here. Wherever boundaries are transgressed, love and hope become flesh there. Said differently, the incarnation is the transgression of boundaries. This new understanding of Christ as the one who transgresses boundaries has radical implications for our Christian witness today.

Understanding Christ beyond boundaries invites us to embark on new voyages of crossing over. In the biblical narratives, the praxis of faith involves new journeys: leaving behind comfort zones to venture into new journeys into the unknown. Each new journey of faith is a transgression of boundaries as we live out a counter-narrative through our leap of faith. Since acts of transgression are illegitimate to the morality of the prevailing order, voyages of crossing over are rife with wind and storm. That is why we are taught and conditioned from our childhood to remain in our comfort zones and domesticate our calling so that we can lead a life in accordance with the standards of the prevailing order. To be present at the bleeding points of history, where we see Christ's self-revelation, involves the boldness of faith to transgress boundaries. This courage is founded on faith in the possibility of a beyond of the prevailing order, inaugurated in the life and ministry of Jesus Christ.

Despite the flood of news channels and print media, the ongoing neo-imperial genocide in our history does not seem to affect us. The rise in death toll in war zones does not prick our conscience. Just like Rachel of Ramah weeping for her children, refused to be consoled because they are no more, the other side of the shore is surrounded with the wailing of mothers who have lost their children to the aggression of the empire. Indoctrinated by the hegemony of the empire, we too legitimise the empire's occupation and invasion in the name of preemptive war and ignore the massacre of innocent children by calling it collateral damage. Ours is a generation converted by the gospel of the empire. For us empire is the eternal truth.

We who have lost the ability to dream visions of alternatives are nothing but a demon-possessed generation. An encounter with Jesus who is beyond the boundaries is the starting point of a new faith journey. This encounter will launch the beginning of a new praxis—a leap of faith—where we engage in transgressing boundaries to clean the land and communities possessed by demons. Redeeming the present times from the clutches of the empire is the contemporary challenge of Christian discipleship. It begins with our Damascus experience.

Endnotes

[1] Larry Rasmussen, "Epiphany," *The Lutheran* 19, no. 1 (January 2006): 23.

4

From Texts of Domestication to Celebration of Apostolicity

Luke 10: 38-42

How do we address a situation when a biblical text considered as authoritative by the church and the faith community is perceived to conflict with our ethical and political convictions? How do we handle texts that seem irredeemable? This is the question that bothers us even as we engage with the story of Martha, Mary and Jesus narrated in Luke 10: 38-42. Religious tradition and Scripture often perpetuate patriarchy through stereotypical images of the ideal Christian woman. Faithful women internalise such gender role models with utmost devotion, and knowingly or unknowingly become passive agents of patriarchy. The question we need to ask here is whether we should maintain the integrity of the text at the expense of the integrity of commitments outside and beyond the text? This reflection is a fragmented response to these questions.

A familiar story from our Sunday school days, we find this text in Luke's Gospel. The evangelist placed this story as part of the travel narrative of Jesus. This story seems to have a positive message for women. "I've been Martha all my life: Now it's my turn to be Mary." This was the response of a woman who got the courage to move beyond the imposed role of domestic helper to engage in activities considered dignified along with men. In the Lukan narrative, we come across an autonomous household, where the sisters make decisions and execute them without the instructions or supervision of a brother or a father or a husband. Mary is portrayed in this text as a courageous woman who crossed the boundaries set by the patriarchal order to become a disciple of Jesus. As a result, we often read this episode as a liberating text in which Jesus invites women to engage in public activities, leaving behind household chores.

It is in such contexts of ambiguity that feminist hermeneutics cautions us to use the hermeneutics of suspicion before venerating the story as a liberating text for women and other communities who experience marginalisation and vulnerability because of their social location. Let us investigate how and why the text constructs the story of these two women as it does. What is the message that this story conveys to the readers? Mary is elevated in the text by humiliating Martha. If Mary has chosen the good portion, then Martha's choice must be at least not good, if not bad. But the fundamental question that we need to raise is: Why do we think that Mary is the ideal model for Christian women in our times?

In our popular expositions of this text, we approach the text in terms of a good woman-bad woman binary. Mainstream Catholic interpretations give women the choice of two lifestyles in their spiritual life: active or contemplative. Women can be either laywomen or nuns, serving their husbands or serving the Lord respectively. In the Protestant tradition, the text is generally interpreted to encourage women to be faithful to their duties as housekeepers along with fulfilling their religious obligations. We see this approach in the programmes of the women's fellowships of Protestant churches. Breakfast sales and intercessory prayer meetings form a part of that.

However, a feminist hermeneutics of suspicion would ask us to discern this text differently. How can we consider this story as a feminist liberative text when Mary who receives positive approval is the silent woman, and Martha, who argues in her own interest, is silenced and ridiculed? Further, the model of discipleship articulated through Mary includes only listening, not engagement and proclamation. The Bible is a sacred text with several stories pitting sister against sister to legitimise patriarchal interests and projects. A hermeneutics of suspicion enables us to understand the toxicity of such texts and their interpretations and encourages us to explore alternative meanings and interpretations that are truly liberative.

Hermeneutics of remembrance is yet another feminist hermeneutical tool to uncover both the values inscribed in the text and the patriarchal or liberative interests of its historical rendering and contextual interpretation. Feminist biblical scholars such as Elizabeth Schussler Fiorenza[1] are of the opinion that this text was generated by and addressed to a situation in the life of the early church, rather than it being an episode in the life of Jesus. For them, the historical context of the text is that of the early Christian community which gathered in house-churches under the leadership of women disciples.

The fourth Gospel testifies that both Martha and Mary were well-known apostolic figures in the early Christian community. In John 11 we read that they were Jesus' friends whom he loved. The climax of the episode of the raising of Lazarus is the Christological confession that Martha makes: "Yes, Lord,

I believe that you are the Messiah, the Son of God, the one coming into the world" (John 11:27). Martha proclaims the messianic faith of the Johannine community which is similar to the confession of Peter at Caesarea Philippi. In other words, we see a parallel between Martha and Peter, and their roles in their respective communities.

It is also important to note the Greek word that is used to describe Martha's activity that Jesus criticised: "She was distracted with much serving" (Luke 10: 40). *Diakonian* and *diakonein* are the words translated as serving in this text. We tend to understand the meaning of serving here as serving at the table. *Diakonia* is a term used several times in Luke and Acts of the Apostles, but it is not used to represent kitchen activity. As we read in Acts 6, the term *diakonia* refers both to the social or Eucharistic ministry to the widows as well as to the preaching of the Word on behalf of the church. So *diakonia* is not a word that designates a person of inferior status involved in domestic work; rather, it represents authorised persons or agents engaged in the ministry of the Christian community. Let us therefore assume that Martha was not distracted by her domestic chores; rather, as a leader of the house church, she was busy with her ministry of serving, teaching and preaching in her community.

The Bible testifies to Mary as a true disciple. We read in John 11 that she had many followers and she enabled them to come to Jesus. Of course, in the narrative of the raising of Lazarus, Mary plays a subordinate role to Martha. But in chapter 12 she anoints Jesus. Unlike the Lukan narrative, in John, the two sisters are not seen in competition with each other.

The hermeneutics of remembrance thus helps us to understand the significant role that women played in the early Christian community along with men. Such discernment invites us to look critically at the Lukan text which pits the apostolic women of the Jesus movement against each other and uses Jesus' words to restrict women's ministry and authority. So we infer that the Lukan episode is not an incident from Jesus' public ministry affirming women's role in the life of the church, but that it is a patriarchal project of the early church to silence and humiliate women leaders like Martha of the house-churches by exalting the silent and subordinate role of Mary. In our engagement with sacred texts, we need to have to be able to distinguish between the Word of God and the word of the establishment.

This discernment is of great significance in our context where we continue to legitimise the silencing and exclusion of women by our interpretations of scripture and tradition. Churches in the Orthodox tradition always use Tradition to perpetuate the exclusion of women from the total life of the church. A recent article on women's choirs established by St. Ephrem in the Ancient Syriac Church reveals that Ephrem considered these women as teachers (*malpanyatha*) of the church engaging in doctrinal instructions, which is higher than the calling of a priest in the Orthodox tradition. To put it differently, ortho-doxy (right belief) was faithfully transmitted over the generations through the agency of women.

Further, Jacob of Serug in his *Homily on St. Ephrem*, a fourth century work, affirms the liberative potential of women's choir.

> Our sisters also were strengthened by you O Ephrem to give praise, for women were not allowed to speak in church. Your instruction opened the closed mouths of the daughters of Eve. A new sight of women uttering the proclamation. And behold they are called teachers among the congregations. Your teaching signifies an entirely new world; For younder in the kingdom, men and women are equal.[2]

This is the story of the Eastern Orthodox Church in the third century. But where are we in the twenty-first century when it comes to women's role in ministry? Why do we not see or refer to such liberative texts when we speak about tradition?

It is in this context that feminist hermeneutics invites us to engage in the hermeneutics of creative imagination which articulates alternative liberating interpretations that reject the patriarchal motives of the text. It enables women to reclaim the biblical text by entering into the text with the help of historical imagination. Such retellings allow us to discard messages that divide, subordinate and alienate one sister from another. They further enable us to engage with the contemporary reality of patriarchal oppression, subordination and silencing in our times through our organic participation in the struggles of women. Liberating biblical women from scriptural captivity and affirming their apostolicity serves as an inspiration for the struggles of contemporary Christian women to make the church an *Ekklesia* of equals and disciples.

Endnotes

[1] Elizabeth Schussler Fiorenza. "A Feminist Critical Interpretation for Liberation: Martha and Mary: Luke 10:38-42." *Religion and Intellectual Life*, vol. 3, no. 2. Winter 1986, pp. 21-36.

[2] https://hugoye.bethmardutho.org/article/hv8n2harvey

5

Parable of the
not-so-Prodigal Daughters

Luke 15: 11-32

The parable of the "prodigal son" is a popular text for preaching and Bible studies. This reflection is an attempt to reread the story from the perspective of the invisible characters—the prostituted women—in this story (15:30). Interestingly, these characters are not mentioned in the main plot or by the main characters. They are only mentioned casually by the older brother and that too by way of the usual stereotypes associated with prostitution. The text is excited about the conversion of the prodigal son, but it does not analyse and critique the system that dehumanised him. The son, irrespective of his actions, was pardoned and taken back to his father's house.

Let us narrate this story from the perspective of those prostitutes, whose lives and bodies were used and exploited by the young and rich men. If given a voice, they would have perhaps said, "Yes, of course, we remember this young man. He was part of a group of youngsters who came to our city. They had lots of money. They had real fun in the city. This young man spent several nights with us. Once he spent all his money, he decided to go back to his father. His father accepted him." Stopping the narration at this stage would be like canonising the events in the story. Let us extend the narrative and enable the young women to speak out and represent themselves:

> We came here not out of our choice. Many of us were sent by our parents to work in the city hoping that our family would then survive. Some men, who guaranteed us jobs, took money from our parents and imprisoned us in this brothel. It was a shock for us when we realised the truth. But we decided to stay and endure this, for the survival of our families. It is next to impossible to escape from here. Some of our friends who attempted to escape were brutally tortured. Even if we succeeded in escaping from here, who will accept us? We don't have a father like the father of the young man who is willing to welcome us back home. We don't have a society that accepts us as fellow beings. We don't have a religious community that provides us fellowship. We are the outcasts, the socially ostracised. We are the lost ones, without the possibility of being found. We are not prostitutes; we are prostituted women; prostituted not only by individual men, but also by an oppressive system of hierarchical and patriarchal power relations, its morality and religiosity.

It is quite interesting to explore why this group of prostituted women are made invisible both from the biblical narrative and from the proclamation of the Word. Is the parable's motive to speak about just saving the prodigal son? Does it not seem that the inclusion of the prostitutes in this story was a deliberate attempt to enhance the sinfulness of the young man and to portray the intensity and depth of the forgiveness that the father granted his son? Is salvation a rescue operation of young rich men from sinful women? What about the "not-so-prodigal daughters" who have been forced into such a situation? The rich young man had the luxury to come back home. He was redeemed. Is there a "Father" who is deeply concerned about the systems that make women prostitutes, and committed to the redemption of those systems and its victims?

> I write to you because I miss you.... I am not working as a servant, but as a prostitute. Each day I must serve 7-8 men. I may get diseases like VD, TB, or AIDS. They threaten to beat me up if I don't do it. They beat up girls who refused them, until they died. They won't take us to be treated because they are afraid that we will run away. Instead they give us two or three tablets.... Being a prostitute is like being a bird in a cage. They can't fly away.[1]

This is not an isolated story. This is the life experience of thousands of poor women and girls who have been "exported" to different countries on account of the growing global market economy that force open the markets of poor countries. "The link between prostitution and global economic injustice and the market economy is increasingly recognized, and it was recently said that a poor nation's most marketable commodity is its women."[2]

Religion plays a significant role in perpetuating prostitution as a necessary evil. Prostitution was accepted as a necessary evil from the early period of Christianity. It is a fact that religion plays a significant role in building social attitudes towards women's bodies and sex which is translated into legislation. Teachers of the church, like Thomas Aquinas, believed that prostitutes, in a way, were permitted by God to prevent chaotic eruptions of sinful male lust. They assumed that prostitutes protected "good" wives from the immoral, lustful demands of their husbands. At the same time, they believed that prostitutes exhibited the sexual licentiousness inherent in all women, inherited from Eve, which "good women" repressed.[3]

Biblical history reveals that the Bible maintained a system of keeping prostituted women as tricksters, harlots, queens, priestesses, and concubines. Tamar, Rahab, Gomer, Jezebel and the woman who anointed Jesus are some among them who came from different empires, cultural backgrounds, languages and cultures. They were the objects of imperial projects of the coloniser. They were not only ignored and made invisible, but their lives were torn and destroyed.

Luke's Gospel is unique in terms of its narrative and theological themes and its presentation of Jesus as a compassionate friend of the outcasts. The heart of Luke's Gospel is a record of mighty acts and teachings of Jesus in solidarity with the outcasts. Luke divides the ministry of Jesus into three periods: the ministry in Galilee, the ministry en route to Jerusalem, and the ministry in Jerusalem. This text comes under the travel narrative, the ministry of Jesus on his way to Jerusalem. One of the most emphatic themes of Luke is his affirmation of the universality of salvation in Christ. When the Pharisees and scribes see tax collectors and sinners coming to Jesus, they grumble and complain that Jesus welcomes and eats with sinners. The famous collection of parables in chapter 15 is a response to that complaint. The parables of the lost sheep, the lost coin and the prodigal son share the common theme of recovery and return of the lost and the alienated. So, it is important to situate this parable along with the other two parables that explain Jesus' solidarity with the last, the least and the lost.

In this parable, the conversation is initiated by the younger son. "Father, give me my share of the estate" (15:12). Without any argument, the father gives the younger son the money he wants. The younger son spends all his money with a group unidentified in the text. He was "dying of hunger," (v17) while his father's servants had enough to spare. Out of hunger and starvation, this son decides to go back. He decides to repent, and the father accepts him with love and compassion. The older brother's response clearly shows that he was very angry with the father and his brother. It is the older brother who complains that the younger brother was devouring his property with the prostitutes.

No doubt the father is concerned about the healing and the restoration of both his sons. However, the thrust of the parable is to articulate the reversal of priority in the reign of God. It is the 'last' that matters. It is the 'insignificant' that brings in joy and happiness. It is the 'silenced' and the represented that make the banquet a possibility. Jesus' commitment to bring back to life those who are lost, and dead, is hence more than an act of benevolence and paternalism. By affirming the colonised, Jesus opens the possibility for them to contest the images inscribed on them and to venture into new journeys creating new selves, "rememorate" their life stories. Unfortunately, the biblical narrative and our proclamation of the Word do not recognise the women who had to sell their bodies for survival. This reality challenges us to analyse critically the various factors that prevent us from hearing the voices of the prostituted women in this parable. When women from debt-ridden countries, whose bodies are the last colonies, read this text, it empowers them to strive for self-worth as they experience a God who is Emmanuel in their midst.

Let us try to analyse this text from a postcolonial, Dalit womanist perspective. This text underscores the postcolonial position that the Bible is an imperial text. Imperialism operates by constructing the other as evil to legitimise and perpetuate a system of domination and hierarchically structured power relations. It would be naïve to see this parable as an innocent and simple story. A simplistic reading of the parable points to some of the myths that the dominant system and its morality give us as reasons for poverty. Why did the younger son have to leave his home? Why did he revolt against the status quo in the family and demand his share? Mary Ann Beavis, in her interpretation of this parable, points to the possibility of an abusive relationship of the father.[4] Another possibility is the undemocratic and unjust power relations within the household economy. In the Indian context, imperialism and caste system have always blamed the rebellion and resistance of the colonised and Dalits against the status quo as the primary reason for their socioeconomic and political disempowerment.

Looking at the text from a Dalit womanist perspective reveals that the idea of purity and pollution is a dominant motif here. As we often tend to think, disobedience is not the real issue here. The younger son became prodigal through his contact with "polluted beings": the prostituted women and pigs. "So he went and hired himself out to one of the citizens of the country, who sent him to his fields to feed the pigs" (15:15). The young man worked with people who were destined to engage in impure and polluting professions because of their race/caste. Again, his co-workers are invisible in the text. However, the motif is clear and visible. What is implied is that contact with the impure and the polluted is sin, and that will alienate us from both the earthly father and the heavenly father. People like the young women in the parable and the co-workers of the young man were not just silenced; they were constructed as inherently impure and sinful. They are more sinned against than sinning. This is the context in which a postcolonial Dalit womanist reading affirms the power of rememorating to rebel against imperial and casteist representations and to construct new 'selves' based on Dalit *testimonios*.

The presence of the prostituted women in this parable can be considered as a layer that is meant to intensify the sinfulness of the young man. It is the story of a household. Interestingly, but not surprisingly, we do not find any female characters in this story, namely the mother or sisters or daughters or wives or even maids. The very absence of household female characters and the presence of prostitutes underscore that this imperial text sees women as symbols of evil and sin.

Having said this, how do women read this text as one of resistance against contemporary manifestations of imperialism? The very realisation that the Bible is an imperial text is in itself liberative for these women, as it enables them to become suspicious about the way the doctrine of the authority of the Bible has been used to suppress their humanity. It also helps them to realise that a new meaning is constructed when their mutilated and colonised bodies become sites of a discursive engagement with the biblical text.

A postcolonial, Dalit womanist reading of this text will focus on a reading from the perspective of the "not-so-prodigal daughters." The bias of God's salvation towards the last, the least and the lost at the expense of the 'better ones' provides new meaning and hope to Dalit women because it affirms their agency. Moreover, the way Jesus did uphold the humanity of prostituted women (John 8:7) gives them a new meaning of fellowship and community. Unlike the story of the prodigal son, Jesus did not send the prostituted woman back to the patriarchal family; rather, he let her anoint him, and affirmed her self-worth and agency in the expansion of the reign of God. A postcolonial, Dalit womanist reading, therefore, must engage in creating imaginative histories and testimonies that create new selves.

> A certain young woman ran away from her father's house to a new city. She went to college, married, divorced. She became successful, and many people knew her name. But she was full of sadness, anger and shame, and she didn't know why. Sometimes she starved herself, sometimes she ate too much, to punish herself for the pain and emptiness she felt inside.
>
> One day, she came to herself and remembered that her father had abused her. She learned to trust these memories. She realised that she had no reason to be ashamed, and that her father had sinned against her! The evil spell that had possessed her was broken, and now she could be free.
>
> When her father died, she returned to the house that had been his. She told her mother what her father had done to her. Her mother believed her, and apologised for pretending not to see, for not protecting her. She embraced her daughter tenderly, weeping, and from that day on, the daughter and her mother became closer.
>
> I tell you, the angels of God rejoice more over when one innocent person survives, than over the repentance of the sinners who have abused them![5]

Endnotes

[1] Aruna Gnanadason, *No Longer a Secret,* (Geneva: WCC, 1993), 19.

[2] Ibid.,17

[3] Rita Nakashima Brock, "Marriage Troubles" in www.panaawtm.org

[4] Mary Ann Beavis, "'Making up Stories': A Feminist Reading of the Parable of the Prodigal Son (Lk. 15: 11b-32)" in Mary Ann Beavis (ed.) *The Lost Coin: Parables of Women, Work and Wisdom* (London: Sheffield Academic Press, 2002), 98-122.

[5] An alternative parable composed by Mary Beavis loosely based on Sylvia Fraser's autobiographical novel, *My Father's House: A Memoir of Incest and Healing.* Beavis. Op cit., 122.

6

Come Holy Spirit;
Transform the Creation

Genesis 1: 1-2

The word Pentecost comes from the Greek word *Pentekoste*, which means fiftieth. In the Jewish tradition it is the feast of weeks, a harvest festival observed on the fiftieth day from the Paschal Feast. In the Christian tradition, Pentecost Sunday is observed on the seventh Sunday after Easter to commemorate the descent of the Holy Spirit on the apostles and the gathered community in Jerusalem after the ascension of Jesus.

God created the universe, and God found it good and beautiful. But this beautiful creation of God has lost its beauty and integrity because of human sinfulness, manifested in greed, exploitation and plunder of the earth, and in consumer culture. Today, even children are familiar with terms such as erratic weather conditions, air pollution, water pollution and global warming. Ecological crisis or climate change is no longer a concept or a prediction; rather, it is an everyday reality.

India is one of the most beautiful countries in the world. But the state of the environment gives us a different picture. The floods in recent years in Tamil Nadu, Mumbai (in Maharashtra) and Kerala is just an example of the state of the environment in India. Floods and droughts have become frequent in recent years. Food security is at stake. Citizens of Bangalore (in Karnataka) stare at a future of acute water scarcity. Many of the world's most air-polluted cities are in India. India has almost 50 million internally displaced people, uprooted from their abodes and livelihoods owing to climate change and development projects.

This is the context in which we reflect on the theme, 'Come Holy Spirit; Transform the Creation!' In fact, we need to reflect upon our ecological sins. We need to confess our carbon sins. The sins of greed and consumerism that we commit knowingly and unknowingly. We need to realise that our lifestyle choices are destroying God's beautiful creation and killing innocent people and other species.

Why are we as Christians concerned about the destruction of the earth? Why do we worry about climate change and the ecological crisis? Is there any connection between creation and the Holy Spirit? These are some of the questions that we need to ask even as we reflect upon the theme "Come Holy Spirit; Transform the Creation."

Holy Spirit is the Life-giving Spirit that Transforms Chaos into Cosmos

The Hebrew word for Spirit is *Ruah*, and it is used in different places in the Old Testament. *Ruah*'s meanings include 'Spirit,' 'breath' and 'wind'. *Ruah* is introduced in the Old Testament as the life-giving Spirit of God. *Ruah* is the breath of God. In the creation narratives in the book of Genesis, we see the

Spirit of God present in the divine act of creation. As we read in Genesis 1 verses one and two, "In the beginning when God created the heavens and the earth, the earth was a formless void, and darkness covered the face of the deep, and the Spirit of God was hovering over the waters." It can also be translated as, the Spirit of God *moved over, hovered over* and *brooded over* the waters. What is the significance of these words used in the creation story to narrate the activity of the Spirit? These words, moving over, brooding over or hovering over, signify that like a mother bird brooding over or hovering over her eggs to bring forth life, the Spirit of God was also involved in the process of giving birth to new life.

According to the Genesis narrative, the context of creation was chaotic. The earth was formless, void and darkness covered the face of the deep. These negative terms describe the context as a tragic, lifeless and death-like situation, and it is in this situation that the Spirit of God enters into the story. In the context of chaos and darkness, the role of the Spirit is not to rebuke or to condemn the situation, but to move over/hover as a mother bird broods over her eggs. So, the vocation of the Spirit of God is to create life amid death and darkness. This biblical witness is the foundation upon which we pray, 'Come Holy Spirit; Transform the Creation'. We are in a tragic and chaotic situation, and we see only death and darkness around us. But we know that the Spirit of God is not a Spirit that condemns God's creation; but it is a Spirit that hovers over creation and transforms them to have life in abundance. So, let us pray together 'Come Holy Spirit; Transform the Creation!'

Holy Spirit is the Groaning Spirit: The Co-Sufferer and the Source of New Life

God created the cosmos from chaos through the work of the life-giving Spirit. But this beautiful cosmos has become chaotic because of human greed and sinfulness. Creation groans because of ecological destruction. Paul, in his epistle to the church in Rome, observes that the whole Creation is groaning for redemption from bondage to decay. "For the creation was subjected to futility, not of its own will but by the will of the one who subjected it, in hope that the creation itself will be set free from its bondage to decay and will obtain the freedom of the glory of the children of God. We know that the whole creation has been groaning in labour pains until now; and not only the creation, but we ourselves, who have the first fruits of the Spirit, groan inwardly while we wait for adoption, the redemption of our bodies. Likewise, the Spirit helps us in our weakness; for we do not know how to pray as we ought, but that very Spirit intercedes with sighs too deep for words," (Romans 8:20). Yes, Creation is groaning for redemption from its present state of decay. But for Paul, it is not just Creation that is crying. Even the Spirit of God is also deeply affected by the ecological crisis. Paul describes the pain and groaning of the Spirit as silent sighs that are too deep for words. This unutterable groaning of the Spirit reveals the depth of God's pain at the destruction of the earth.

What do we gather from this rather disturbing narration about the groaning of the Spirit and the pain of God? First, it is not God who causes the destruction of the earth; rather it is the consequence of human sinfulness. God is angry, God is upset, and God is deeply pained by our actions which desecrate God's beautiful creation. So, the Spirit of God is a co-sufferer with creation. Second, for Paul, the groaning of Creation is not a cry that precedes death, but a groaning in labour that precedes new life. That is why Paul uses the metaphor of labour pain to describe the groaning of Creation. The Spirit of God experiences the pain of creation, and the Spirit too groans with Creation. At the same time, the Spirit of God instils hope in the community of Creation and transforms the groaning into a labour pain, anticipating the birth of new life amid death and destruction. Even as we mourn the destruction of the earth, let us be assured of the promise of God to redeem Creation. So, let us pray together 'Come Holy Spirit; Transform the Creation!'

Holy Spirit is the Empowering Spirit of Transformation

Our biblical expositions help us to understand the Holy Spirit as the life-giving Spirit that transforms chaos into cosmos. We have realised that the Holy Spirit is a co-sufferer with Creation and yet it instils in them the hope with which to transform their groaning into the birth of new life. But the Holy Spirit requires partners to continue the vocation of transforming Creation. Genesis 2 reminds us that the vocation of human beings is to "till and to keep" the earth. It is not to subdue and exploit nature; not to have dominion over Creation. But to 'till and to keep' the earth. That is our vocation and the Holy Spirit anoints us for this vocation.

So, when we pray 'Come Holy Spirit; Transform the Creation', we are not asking the Holy Spirit to clean the mess we have created. Rather, it is a public confession of our ecological sins; the sins that have destroyed the beauty of God's creation. God is pained because of our ecological sins. So, 'Come Holy Spirit; Transform the Creation,' is a prayer of confession and repentance. It is also a prayer of commitment. A prayer that declares our commitment to participate with God in renewing and transforming Creation.

On 24 May 2019, many cities around the world witnessed the 'School Strike 4 Climate'. This is a movement initiated by the young Swedish student Greta Thunberg. In her inspiring address to world leaders she said, "We children are doing this to wake the adults up. We children are doing this because we want our hopes and dreams back."[1] It was this same message that reverberated in our streets when our children firmly declared, "The ocean is rising and so are we."[2] The ecological crisis is a wake-up call for us. For such a time as this we are called to become the tidal wave of hope. "The ocean is rising and so are we."

Endnotes

[1] https://www.joe.co.uk/amp/news/greta-thunberg-speech-to-mps-228919

[2] https://www.stuff.co.nz/environment/climate-news/111089917/climate-change-strike-this-is-why-kiwi-kids-are-bunking-school

7

"And You Renew the Face of the Earth"

Psalm 104: 30

"Praise be to you, my Lord, through our Sister, Mother Earth, who sustains and governs us, and who produces various fruit with coloured flowers and herbs. This sister now cries out to us because of the harm we have inflicted on her by our irresponsible use and abuse of the goods with which God has endowed her. We have come to see ourselves as her lords and masters, entitled to plunder her at will. The violence present in our hearts, wounded by sin, is also reflected in the symptoms of sickness evident in the soil, in the water, in the air and in all forms of life. This is why the earth herself, burdened and laid waste, is among the most abandoned and maltreated of our poor; she 'groans in travail.'" – Pope Francis, *Laudato Si*[1]

Creation Sunday is a time to thank God for the beautiful blue planet and the community of creation. It is also a time to be self-reflexive and examine how we continue to destroy and disfigure God's beautiful creation. It is a time to be inspired by the vision of a redeemed earth and to commit ourselves to ministries of earth-healing and eco-justice in our respective contexts.

Psalm 104 is a beautiful hymn articulating our faith in God, who created the cosmos, and it celebrates life in abundance through mutual dependency. The Psalm also recognises the presence of sin and evil which can distort the beauty and harmony of life that is shared in community. Nevertheless, the Psalm affirms the faith in God's commitment to renew the face of the earth.

God created the world by sharing God's life-giving breath. It is the entire community of Creation—not just human beings— that share the divine breath. Sharing the divine breath means sharing the being of God. Creation is hence God's cosmic embodiment, and in a metaphorical sense, the world is the body of God. This is echoed in Martin Luther as he calls the earth the God-indwelling creation. Pope Francis also reiterates such a panentheistic Creation theology in his encyclical.

> The universe unfolds in God, who fills it completely. Hence, there is a mystical meaning to be found in a leaf, in a mountain trail, in a dewdrop, in a poor person's face. The ideal is not only to pass from the exterior to the interior to discover the action of God in the soul, but also to discover God in all things.[2]

Psalm 104 reminds us that Creation is the microcosm of the Godhead. The Cappadocian interpretation of Trinity, using the term *Pericherosis*, affirms the relationship of mutuality within the Godhead. Trinitarian faith presents God as the one who refuses to be alone. God who finds meaning of life in communion and community. God who is longing for the joy of friendship and fellowship. We see the same *pericherotic* experience in the community of Creation. Psalm 104 challenges the anthropocentric understanding of Creation where human beings are privileged with intrinsic worth over against other creatures. For the psalmist, each creature has its own intrinsic worth, and each creature celebrates its life by being at the service of the other members of the community of Creation. Interdependence and mutuality practised among creatures make life in community a joyous celebration. We see a qualitative difference in the Creation theology and the vocation of human beings in this text compared with the creation narratives in the book of Genesis. The vocation of human beings, according to Genesis 1, is "to subdue the earth and have dominion" over the rest of Creation. Genesis 2 suggests that human vocation is "to till and to keep." But when it comes to Psalm 104, the psalmist talks about the vocation of all creatures, which is mutual dependency and cross-fertilisation.

The Psalm, which portrays the integrity of Creation in romantic language, however, recognises the presence of sin and destruction that curtails the flourishing of life on earth. The psalmist laments: "Let sinners be consumed from the earth, and let the wicked be no more," (Psalm 104:35). The psalmist's engagement with Leviathan in the text (Psalm 104:26) is of profound significance in our contemporary context of ecological crisis. Here the Psalm categorically observes that the ecological crisis is not caused by non-human beings. Even the Leviathan—the primordial symbol of chaos and destruction—is God's friend and companion. References to Leviathan in other biblical books tend to project God's mighty power over the forces of chaos (Isaiah 27:1, Psalm 74:14, Job 41:1). But in our text, Leviathan is simply another creature that delights in the world that God has made. Leviathan's purpose in the created order is "to sport" in the sea. It does not appear here as a frightening creature, but one that "frolics" and plays. Perhaps, God created Leviathan "to play with it." To put it differently, for the psalmist, Leviathan is not a creature God sees as an enemy; rather it is God's friend and partner in making the celebration of joy in the community of Creation a reality. This interpretation of Leviathan calls for an alternative diagnosis of the ecological crisis. Ecological crisis is not a natural calamity that is caused by God. Ecological crisis is the consequence of systemic sin and structural evil. The psalmist helps us to realise the tragic reality that systemic sin coexists with the celebration of life on earth.

As Isaiah reminds us,

> The earth dries up and withers, the world languishes and withers; the heavens languish together with the earth. The earth lies polluted under its inhabitants; for they have transgressed laws, violated statutes, broken the everlasting covenant (Isaiah 24:4-5).

Isaiah's diagnosis of the ecological crisis is still relevant in our times. It is the profit-mongering and corporate greed which privileges profit over life that causes genocide and ecocide in our times. Desecration of the earth is the desecration of the body of God.

As Isaiah prophesied, "God is going to do a new thing on earth" (Isaiah 43:19). The psalmist reaffirms the same hope in God: "God is going to renew the face of the earth" (Psalm 104:30). Alternatives are possible. A redeemed earth is God's promise for the community of Creation.

The church came into being on Pentecost day, with the sending of the breath of God. Creation is a Pentecost experience. When creatures with diverse natures, temperament and outlook are filled with the life-giving breath of God, a community of Creation becomes a reality, in spite of the differences and diversity. If creation is a Pentecost experience, earth is the sanctuary, and all of us are members of this cosmic body of Christ. In the midst of the ecological crisis, we are called to be God's partners in renewing the face of the earth. The church is called to become the divine breath in the valleys of dry bones and to celebrate the joy of life in the community. In the context of corporate plunder of God's beautiful world and the subaltern communities, we are called to be a disturbing presence so that through our ministries of earth-healing, the face of the earth will be renewed. "When you send forth your spirit, they are created; and you renew the face of the ground" (Psalm 104:30).

Endnotes

[1] http://w2.vatican.va/content/dam/francesco/pdf/encyclicals/documents/papa-francesco_20150524_enciclica-laudato-si_en.pdf

[2] http://w2.vatican.va/content/dam/francesco/pdf/encyclicals/documents/papa-francesco_20150524_enciclica-laudato-si_en.pdf

8

All Creation Groans: Healing of the Earth

Romans 8: 18-27

A few years ago, the *New Internationalist* magazine ran a story about a group of angry monkeys blocking traffic in a busy highway in eastern Uganda when a female member of the troop was killed by a speeding truck. They surrounded her body in the middle of the highway and held a 'sit-in,' refusing to move for about 30 minutes, blocking the highway completely.

The groaning of creation is everywhere. But we have become used to living with such haunting cries and we pretend as if everything is fine with us. Discerning the signs of the times is a faith imperative. It demands from us the commitment to listen and to problematise the groaning so that we respond meaningfully and relevantly to God's call.

How do we problematise the groaning of Creation? The monkeys in the *New Internationalist* news story compel us to go beyond our dominant perception to re-imagine groaning as public protest. The groaning of creation that we encounter in our daily life is an invitation to transgress the boundaries of our analytical horizons to problematise what we see and hear so that we understand the world differently.

Groaning is a metaphor extensively used in biblical texts to signify the diversity of existential realms (Exodus 2:24; 6:5; Judges 2:18; Job 23:2; Psalm 6:6; Isaiah 21:2; Jeremiah 45:3, Acts 7:34; Romans 8:22, et al). Groaning portrays the pathos, the experience of God-forsakenness, the discernment of unjust social relations, envisioning of alternatives, revolutionary patience for the unfolding of utopia, and the radical experiences of epiphany. So, from a biblical perspective, groaning indicates the presence of deep-rooted sin and injustice in the social fabric.

As we learn from biblical texts, groaning is also 'God talk'. Confronted with the experience of utter God-forsakenness, the community of creation reimagines God, inspired by the surprising encounters of epiphanies at the most unexpected places. Groaning discerns God differently as a co-sufferer who laments with people while keeping their hope alive.

How do we discern the groaning of creation in our times? What are the insights that we gather from such groaning even as we strive to reflect upon our mission and ministry in the context of climate injustice?

Groaning: A Critique of Structural Sin and Injustice

As in the monkey story, groaning exposes the structural sin and injustice that perpetuate death and destruction. A public display of the violent face of our prevailing order questions the very diagnosis of the problem and the solutions prescribed by experts. Groaning as a social protest calls for counter-engagements with the problem that leads to new diagnosis informed by the experiences of the victims. So, groaning proposes two things: a suspicion of the dominant narratives of the problem and their solutions, and the cognitive potential of the experiences of the communities destined to depart "before their time." Differently said, groaning is a discourse emerging from the counter-public spheres of our times and that proposes a new epistemological key to discern the signs of the times.

In the story of our ancestors narrated in the book of Genesis, the Lord said to Cain, "Your brother's blood is crying out to me from the ground. And now you are cursed from the ground…. When you till the ground, it will no longer yield to you its strength" (Genesis 4: 10-12). Fratricide and ecocide are integrally connected. The eco-crisis that we confront in this story is both the refusal and the inability of the land to yield fruits when there is blood on the hands of the tiller and keeper. To put it differently, the ecological crisis is more than a change in the mercury level. When the harmonious relationship in the community of creation that was found as good by the Creator is disrupted due to arrogance, greed, domination, power and accumulation, creation is robbed of its integrity and agency, and it is reduced into the state of a commodity to be exploited, manipulated and sold for profit. So, the groaning of the blood of Abel emerging from the land is a mirror held up to our sinful worldview and structures that prevent us from becoming siblings and neighbours to the community of creation.

In the same book, we come across a similar weeping by a single mother who is raped and dispossessed by Abraham (Genesis 21: 15-19). Denied of the right over property and inheritance, Hagar and Ishmael are wandering in the wilderness and are crying for water. Water is a basic human right, and its denial is a sin against humanity. In our world today, we come across different manifestations of desert experiences, where we hear the groaning for water every day. When water becomes a commodity with a price tag, Hagars and Ishmaels are destined to die in the wilderness without access to drinking water. The groaning in the wilderness compels us to question whether water crisis is a natural calamity or not. The weeping of Hagar and Ishmael provides us with a lens to understand the contemporary crisis of water. The intimate violence on a slave woman's body and the subsequent disinheritance of both her and her son from their legitimate property rights are integrally related with the desert experience and cry for water by Hagar and Ishmael. Accumulation is possible only through dispossession, and the dispossessed are the ones who groan for water in our world today. We meet them today in our own communities where people are uprooted and dispossessed from their livelihood and life world.

Groaning does not end with Genesis; it continues in the book of Exodus as well. "The Israelites groaned under their slavery and cried out. Out of the slavery their cry for help rose up to God" (Exodus 2:23). Groaning emerging from the context of slavery affirms the inalienability of human dignity and human rights. Human beings, as created in the image of God, are not meant to live as slaves. Slavery is the negation of God because it takes away the God-given right to freedom and adequate rest (Sabbath) to God's creation. The groaning of the slaves exposes the inherent sinfulness and injustice of the imperial order. While the Egyptian Empire diagnosed the shortage in production as a result of the laziness of the slaves, the slaves exposed it as injustice.

Imperial violation of human dignity is not a story that we read in history books alone. It is also a contemporary reality. When workers are exploited in sweat shops, Special Economic

Zones, and in the contract sector without the protection of labour laws and the right to organise, we hear their groaning exposing the sinfulness of the system. In such contexts, groaning is a public protest, unveiling the brutal face of neoliberal capitalism and imperialism.

In the prophetic books we again encounter the groaning of God's creation for freedom and dignity. Isaiah narrates the outcry in the streets where joy has reached its eventide (Isaiah 24: 1-13). "How long will the land mourn?" Jeremiah cries aloud (Jeremiah 12:4). In the book of Joel, even wild animals cry out to God because their water and food supply has dried up (Joel 1: 17-20). In these texts we see the portrayal of the groaning and lamentation of the whole community of creation—the land, the grain, and the cattle. They groan because the earth has become desolate. This reality of desolation is the consequence of sin and injustice. As Isaiah puts it, "the earth lies polluted under its inhabitants; for they have transgressed the laws, violated the statutes, and broken the everlasting covenant" (Isaiah 24:5). In short, the groaning of the earth community that reverberates from biblical narratives is a counterargument uncovering the sinfulness and injustice inherent in the human projects of conquest and accumulation.

Groaning: New Experiences of Epiphany

Groaning of creation is more than a public protest; it is also a public witness of the God whom the wounded Creation continues to meet amid their sufferings and struggles. When confronted with the sway of death which takes away their life and livelihood, people often cry aloud, "My God, my God, why have your forsaken us?" Ecological crises which lead to pauperisation, deforestation, displacement, climate change, exile, and social unrest and violence are experiences of utter God-forsakenness. The victims have been told that eco-crisis is God's punishment for their iniquities. It is in this context of God-forsakenness and distorted God-talk that the victims encounter new epiphanies, experiencing God as a co-sufferer who keeps their hopes alive. Such experiences of new epiphanies enable them to reimagine God afresh in the context of eco-crisis. Groaning of creation, therefore, articulates an alternative imagination of God.

In Romans 8, Paul talks about the groaning of the whole creation for freedom from bondage and decay. The climax of this narrative is the groaning of the Spirit. In the sigh of the Spirit we see and hear the pain of God. God's pain is described as silent sighs that are too deep for words. In other words, the unutterable groaning of the Spirit reveals the depth of God's pain. It is an extension of God's passion which we see on the cross. If the Spirit of God is hurt and groaning because of the suffering of the community of creation, God continues to suffer because of ecological sins caused by our prevailing social relations.

In the Genesis narrative of the murder of Abel we see the pain of God; a God who is wounded by human sinfulness which leads to death and destruction. The dominant reading of this story tells us that God cursed Cain for his sinfulness. "And now you are cursed from the ground…When you till the ground, it will no longer yield to you its strength," (Genesis 4:12). A deeper engagement with the text and the groaning of God will help us see and read this text differently. God is neither cursing Cain nor commanding the earth not to yield to its strength when human beings till and cultivate. Rather, God is reminding Cain of the consequences of violence and death which destroy the harmony of the community of creation. To put it differently, God's response to this primordial act of death and destruction is not one of judgment or curse, but one of God inviting Cain to continue to live as God's partner in the ongoing process of creation without infringing the rights of other members of the community of creation.

The biblical narrative of the descendants of Cain is also important here. Cain's son Enoch built a city. His great grandson Jabal was the ancestor of those who live in tents and have livestock (Genesis 4:20). His brother Jubal was the ancestor of all those who play the lyre and pipe (Genesis 4:21). And their cousin Tubal-cain made all kinds of bronze and iron tools (Genesis 4:22). That means the descendants of Cain were people who contributed creatively to the flourishing of creation through their engagement in diverse creative activities such as tent making, animal husbandry, construction work, music and fine arts, and science and technology. What is the God-talk that we find in this narrative? While God is wounded at the violence that was perpetuated on Abel, God is not cursing Cain and destroying him. Rather, God is affirming Cain and his descendants as co-creators with the responsibility to continue the creative process in history.

The Bible testifies that Cain's descendants fulfilled God's expectations through their creative interventions in diverse areas, leading to the flourishing of creation. So, the God whom we reimagine in the groaning of Abel's blood is a God who affirms human potential to participate in God's creative process in spite of human sinfulness. Yes, God is pained by the brutal murder of Abel. God is angry too. God is groaning. But God believes in the possibility of transformation. Sin does not take away our creativity. Despite our sinfulness, we are able to participate in God's creative mission to work for God's creation to flourish.

In the story of the raped and dispossessed single mother Hagar and her son Ishmael, we see the tragic experience of utter God-forsakenness. In the wilderness, confronting death, she "lifted up her voice and wept" (Genesis 21:16). The story tells us that God heard the boy's groaning. Groaning opens and makes possible a new experience of God in the wilderness, God as a well of water. As we read in chapter 16, Hagar named God *El-roi*, which means God who sees. So, for the dispossessed who go through desert experiences, God is ever present as 'wells of water' in their struggles for survival. In our contemporary context of growing desertification and dispossession due to global warming and climate change, the groaning of creation inspires us to re-vision God as 'springs of life' that sustain and nourish us in our struggles against death and destruction.

In the book of Exodus, we have seen the cry of the enslaved people exposing the inherent evil and injustice of the imperial order. The Horeb episode narrates God's encounter with Moses where God appears in a flame of fire out of a bush. The bush was blazing but it was not consumed. Then God revealed Godself as the one who observed and heard the groaning of the enslaved people. This revelation portrays God as organically present in the struggles and sufferings of the community. God is not a distant, transcendent reality detached from the everyday struggles of God's creation; rather, God is very much present amid their struggles as a co-sufferer. It is through God's organic participation in the sufferings and struggles of the community that God enables them to believe in alternatives. God instills in them a new vision of liberation from the shackles of slavery and domination.

The symbol of the burning bush is instructive for us as we confront global warming and climate change. We are all victims of the rise in temperature in different ways. We see burning bushes all around us. *The Intergovernmental Panel on Climate Change (IPCC),* governments, bodies of the United Nations, NGOs and even churches are trying to convince us that climate change is a hazard or a risk that is irreversible. The only option before us is to adapt and and mitigate misery. It is in this context of the indoctrination of the doctrine of "there is no alternative" that we need to revisit the symbol of the burning bush as a site of epiphany. The primordial vision of the burning bush has the audacity to believe that the blazing fire cannot destroy the beauty of the bush. Epiphany empowers us to believe in the possibility of a beyond of the present. The present is not eternal. You do not have to be adapted to the prevailing order. There is still room for hope, and we need to be infected with this hope so that we can make hope contagious. This is the power of epiphany that emerges from the groaning of creation.

Groaning: The Labour Pain for Alternatives

We have seen that the groaning of creation is a public protest and a public witness: a public protest against the unjust and sinful social structures that perpetuate death and destruction and a public witness of the God who is very much present in the midst of our struggles, keeping our hopes alive. Paul provides us yet another unique insight about the groaning of creation: "The whole creation has been groaning in *labour pains*" (Romans 8:22). This imagery of the groaning of creation as labour pains raises fundamental questions regarding our Christian engagement with the ecological crisis. The cry that we hear from the earth and its children is not a groaning that precedes death, but a groaning in labour that precedes new life. The groaning that surrounds us is not the sign of hopelessness and death; rather, it is the proclamation of a new beginning for the community of creation.

Groaning as the labour pain for alternatives, a message of hope for all of us as we face the reign of death in our everyday lives. Ecological crisis should not lead us to withdraw ourselves from our social and political engagements and to prepare ourselves to face impending death and destruction. Rather, ecological crisis invites us to envision a world redeemed of the sinfulness of exploitation, plunder and accumulation, where we experience the fullness of the community of creation. It is such alternative visions that inspire and sustain our struggles against the destruction of the earth and other social evils. When our groaning becomes the labour pain of a redeemed world, we become an Advent community, anticipating in hope the birthing of a new world. Yes, the groaning of Creation is the audacity of hope that believes that "another world is possible."

Climate change campaigns warn us about an impending destruction. All of us experience the impact of global warming in diverse ways in our own communities and our own bodies. We are all in despair, waiting for the impending calamity to devour us. The mood that surrounds us is one of a death vigil for our turn to be sacrificed at the altar of global warming. Until then, through adaptation and mitigation we can postpone the tragedy. But the tragedy is inevitable and irreversible. It is in this context that we fall back on Paul who portrays a different understanding of waiting. For Paul, the creation is eagerly waiting and longing for its redemption from bondage to decay. Paul is not talking about adaptation or some adjustments to live with decay. Paul is affirming the possibility of the very end of decay. So, groaning and waiting for Paul is not a death vigil but a waiting for new life; it is just like waiting outside the labour room of a hospital to welcome the birth of new life. New life is hidden amid death and destruction. But we need the discerning ability to recognise it, the audacity to believe in it, and the revolutionary patience to wait for it.

Our groaning becomes a labour pain for alternatives when we regain the courage, faith and imagination to believe in alternatives. Unfortunately, our scientific and objective knowledge systems do not allow us to dream new visions. We are told that alternatives are not only impossible but also illegitimate. Paul reminds us that "hope that is seen is not hope" (Romans 8:24). What does it mean? The doctrine of "there is no alternative" talks about the hope that is seen. It is realistic, objective and scientific. There are sufficient scientific arguments to prove this. But for Paul that is not hope. "If we hope for what we do not see, we wait for it with patience" (Romans 8:25). So, hope is the hope for what we do not see. This vision of hope is absurd to the logic of our times. Still, Paul invites us to dream this absurd hope because "in hope we were saved" (Romans 8:24). So, the groaning of creation as labour pain for alternatives instills in us this absurd hope that tomorrow can be a different day. With that hope we are invited to be an Advent community, discerning the partial blossoming of that hope in our communities through our ministries of resistance and resilience in healing the world.

9

"Let Everyone who is Thirsty, Come"

Revelation 21:6, 22:17

The Book of Revelation is one of the most misunderstood and distorted books in Christian Scripture. Most end-times writings and preachings are based on this book, reducing it to the level of "God's pre-ordained script of predictions" on the end and destruction of the earth. As a result, we tend to think that the ecological crisis is part of God's plan foretold in the Bible. In the context of climate change, a distorted reading of the apocalyptic literature would make us think that the initiatives of the environmental movements to preserve and protect the planet are against God's plan and purpose. Differently said, our dominant theological and spiritual reflections on the Book of Revelation not only propose ecological destruction as God's will but also instill in us a world-denying faith and spirituality, making us insensitive to the groaning of God's creation for redemption.

A deeper engagement with the Book of Revelation would help us to understand it as a passionate critique of Roman imperial power. It is a critique which unveils the vision of an alternative world in the making—the redeemed earth. Envisioned by the vision of a new heaven and new earth, Revelation further challenges believers to come out of the empire and to proleptically celebrate the experience of the redeemed earth in the worship and service of God who is making all things new. So, Revelation is an outright rejection of our otherworldly faith and spirituality, and it invites us to participate in God's system-threatening politics that transforms Babylon into Jerusalem. In the context of contemporary manifestations of neocolonial invasions and plunder, camouflaged as progress, growth and development, Revelation challenges us to encounter and counter the forces of death and destruction, informed by the vision of the redeemed earth. It further inspires us to look for signs of hope, even when evil seems overpowering.

We are a thirsty people in a parched land. According to World Health Organization, in 2019, one out of every three people in the world lacked access to safe drinking water.[1] In 2017, almost 1.6 million people died from diarrheal diseases globally—the result of unsafe water and sanitation. This is more than all deaths from all 'intentional injuries' combined in the same year: almost 800,000 died from suicide, 405,000 from homicide, 130,000 in conflict, and 26,500 from terrorism.[2] Today's water crisis is not an issue of scarcity, but of access and equitable distribution of water within the community. One toilet flush in the northern hemisphere uses as much water as the average person in the global South uses for a whole day's drinking, cooking, washing and cleaning. A bathtub holds 150 litres of water. But an average slum-dweller in India cannot even think about 150 litres of water for their entire needs for a week. Under globalisation, water has become a commodity with a price tag, and common property resources such as lakes and rivers have been auctioned to multinational corporations to attract foreign capital. This is the context in which we are called to witness to the in-breaking of the New Jerusalem. How do we engage in public witnessing envisioned by the vision of the redeemed earth as we experience the desecration and commodification of life-giving water?

The Book of Revelation is a great resource as we search for discernment in the context of water crisis. Firstly, there is no sea in the vision of the new heaven and the new earth narrated in Revelation 21. "And the first earth had passed away and the sea was no more" (Revelation 21:1). There is no sea in the redeemed earth. This is a disturbing vision. When we struggle together to restore and redeem our waterbodies, John's vision talks about the absence of sea in the new dispensation. How do we understand this vision? John in this chapter gives a series of items that are said to be "no more" in the new city. No more death, no more mourning, and no more weeping and pain. Why is the sea listed in Revelation along with death, pain, tears and mourning? How can we accept the absence of sea in the redeemed earth?

Revelation portrays sea as a political and economic category—the symbol of systemic evil. The disappearance of the sea in New Jerusalem is hence a critique of the political economy of the Roman Empire. The sea made possible the plundering of colonised communities and their land by Roman imperial powers. Babylon's economy was based on long-distance maritime trade in luxury goods. We see the seer's critique of sea trade and shipping in chapter 18. Chapter 18 gives us a detailed account of sea as the locus of evil. In the unjust imperial economy of Rome, "everyone who had ships at sea grew rich by her wealth" (Revelation 18:19). For Babylon, the sea was the primary agent for exercising its might and power—to invade, plunder, destroy, and enslave communities and nature in the colonies. The description of its cargo in chapter 18 reveals how the landscape and the communities at the peripheries were commodified by Rome. "Cargo of gold, silver, jewels and pearls, fine linen, silk and scarlet, all kinds of scented wood, bronze, iron, and myrrh, frankincense, wine, olive oil, choice flour and wheat, cattle and sheep, horses and chariots, slaves and human lives" (Rev 18:11). The very presence of slaves and human lives in the cargo exposes the magnitude of the sinfulness of the imperial political economy.

Imperial power is always built on the colonised bodies of the other—the marginalised communities and the plundered earth. So, the disappearance of sea in the redeemed earth is not the disappearance of water *per se*; rather, it is the alternative vision of a redeemed earth as antithetical to the imperial political economy of greed, commodification and accumulation. Living in the time of globalisation which continues to plunder, privatise and contaminate our waterbodies, the vision of the absence of sea in the redeemed earth is the assurance that our struggles are not in vain.

Secondly, as an alternative to the imperial reality of water as a commodity for profit, in the redeemed earth, water is presented as a gift for all. "To the one who is thirsty I will give to drink from the spring of the water of life as a gift" (Rev 21:6). "Let everyone who is thirsty come. Let everyone who wishes, take the water of life as a gift" (Rev 22: 17). The word *dorean,* which is translated as gift, means without cost or without money. This is an alternative vision of hope for people who lack the purchasing power to buy water. Revelation's vision of the redeemed earth is the vision of a gift economy where God's creation is available to everyone, not just to people with money. This is also a vision of the redemption of our waterbodies—oceans, lakes, rivers, estuaries and wells. This promise of free access to clean and pure water is the divine rejection of the prevailing political economy of privatisation and commodification of water. This vision is also a judgment on all who are insensitive to the cries for water. We see the same vision of an alternative in Isaiah. "When the poor and needy seek water and there is none, I will open rivers on the bare heights, and fountains in the midst of the valleys. I will make the wilderness a pool of water, and the dry land springs of water" (Isaiah 41: 17-18).

Thirdly, the book of Revelation provides us with a vision of the river of the water of life, flowing from the throne of God and of the lamb, through the middle of the street of the city. We see here a new vision of God. God is not a God of judgment and condemnation. Rather, God is a God who is committed to heal the earth. Further, in this vision, healing of the earth does not come directly from God or the lamb; rather healing comes through the leaves of the tree which is nourished by the river of the water of life. For Revelation, redemption is not a reality that is limited to human souls; it is an experience that embraces the entire creation of God. Further, Revelation proclaims an alternative doctrine of salvation when it affirms the agency of leaves and water in the healing of nations. In other words, leaves and waters participate in the divine mission of redemption in history.

These three insights from the book of Revelation highlighted here demand a response from us. We are called to strive towards the disappearance of "sea" in our times. We are called to struggle together to make water a gift for all. We are called to recognise water and leaves as agents of our salvation. A positive response to this call demands from us the courage and commitment to believe in the possibility of a redeemed earth. Revelation gives us the clarion call to "come out" of Babylon. It is a call to get out of the imperial and market-oriented worldview of profit and plunder and to opt for a life-affirming worldview of healing and restoration, in solidarity with the social movements of our times. As Arundhati Roy reminds us,

> Our strategy should be not only to confront empire, but to lay siege to it. To deprive it of oxygen. To shame it. To mock it. With our art, our music, our literature, our stubbornness, our joy, our brilliance, our sheer relentlessness—and our ability to tell our own stories. Stories that are different from the ones we're being brainwashed to believe. The corporate revolution will collapse if we refuse to buy what they are selling—their ideas, their version of history, their wars, their weapons, their notion of inevitability. Remember this: We be many and they be few. They need us more than we need them. Another world is not only possible, she is on her way. On a quiet day, I can hear her breathing.[3]

Endnotes

[1] https://www.who.int/news-room/detail/18-06-2019-1-in-3-people-globally-do-not-have-access-to-safe-drinking-water-unicef-who

[2] https://ourworldindata.org/childhood-diarrheal-diseases

[3] https://www.globalpolicy.org/component/content/article/162-general/27826.html

10

Messianic Politics and Christian Discipleship

Mark 9: 30-37

In the Markan narrative, the reflection on the messianic identity of Jesus is followed by a series of conversations between Jesus and his disciples on messianic politics. The Gospel of Mark is the story of discipleship. So, the discourse on messianic identity and messianic politics is presented in the context of discerning the challenges of following Christ. Further, this discourse takes place "on the way" to Jerusalem. It is on the way of the cross that Jesus enabled his disciples to understand messianic identity and politics, and their implications for discipleship.

The text begins with Jesus talking to his disciples about his betrayal, murder and resurrection. But the disciples fail to understand the meaning of what he was saying and they continue to engage in an argument about who is the greatest among them. When they reach Capernaum, Jesus asks them about their argument. Then he says, "Whoever wants to be first must be last of all and servant of all" (Mark 9:35). Jesus then brings a child to their midst and says, "Whoever welcomes one such child in my name welcomes me, and whoever welcomes me welcomes not me but the one who sent me" (Mark 9: 36-37).

Three times Jesus brings children into the discourse in the Markan account of the messianic politics narrated in chapters 9 and 10. Chapter 9 begins with the experience on the mountain of transfiguration (9: 2-13), and Mark juxtaposes the mountain of transfiguration with the valley of disfiguration by presenting the spirit-possessed deaf-mute boy (9: 14-29). Then, Jesus brings a little child into their midst and proclaims that whoever welcomes one such child in his name welcomes him (9: 36-37). Finally, Jesus becomes indignant and says to his disciples, "Let the little children come to me; do not stop them; for it is to such as these that the kingdom of God belongs" (Mark 10:14)

The metaphor of a child is significant in understanding the messianic politics of Jesus and the implications for our journey of discipleship. We are all familiar with sermons and homilies idealising children as symbols of purity, innocence and trust. This text has also been used to present Jesus as a friend of children, and we are familiar with several songs on how Jesus loves little children. But it is in the context of the discourse on his messianic politics that Jesus is using children as a living metaphor. How do we make sense of it?

In the social world of Jesus, children were the "little ones" without social status and rights. This is the testimony of Mark. In Mark's Gospel, children are presented only in situations of sickness or oppression: the synagogue ruler's daughter (5:21ff.), the Syropheoenician woman's daughter (7:24ff.), and the deaf and dumb son (9:14ff.). From this consistent narrative pattern, we can assume that the Markan metaphor of child represents victims.

It is also important to note that Jesus' affirmation of children as inheritors of the reign of God takes place in a house. In the household, children, along with women, are the primary victims of practices of domination. Children are completely dependent on adults, and their love for adults in the family is used/abused by adults to impose their supremacy over them. Repressive paternalism enables the manipulation of the powerless by the dominant. Also, they are socialised and indoctrinated to internalise the prevailing power relations and hierarchical order. The family system that perpetuates practices of exclusion and domination here stands as a microcosm of the wider society. It is in this context that we need to understand the messianic politics of Jesus and its affirmation of children.

The spirit-possessed child, whom Jesus heals at the foot of the mountain of transfiguration, provides us with a distinct and deeper meaning of Jesus' messianic politics. Here we see a boy possessed by a spirit that renders him speechless. The Markan narrative enables us to see a correlation between the possession of the physical body and the possession of the social body. For example, in the story of the demon-possessed man on the other side of the sea, the name he gives to himself is Legion (Mark 5). Legion refers to the Roman military. The demons came out of the man and entered a herd of swine, and they rushed down the steep bank into the lake and drowned. Interestingly, the word 'herd' was also a synonym for the imperial army. It is significant to note here that the social world of Jesus was entrenched in Roman imperialism. A careful reading of this text enables us to see the correlation between the possession of the physical body and the possession of the social body. In other words, the significance is of casting out oppressive demons from the social body as much as the physical body.

It is in this context that we approach the spirit-possessed boy at the foot of the mountain of transfiguration. The spirit disables his ability to speak. Speechlessness is the issue here. From a postcolonial perspective, the boy who is denied his right to speak provides us with a lens to see communities whose voices are silenced. Once again, we see the correlation between the possession of the physical body and the possession of the social body. So, what is the significance of this silenced boy within the discourse on messianic politics? Messianic politics exposes the forceful silencing of victims and enables the victims to speak out. Jesus is not authorising his disciples to be the voice of the voiceless: rather, he is reclaiming the right of the powerless to speak and thereby to be the subjects of their destiny.

Jesus' attempt in this story is not to present children as meek and mild and to romanticise his friendship with the kids. Children stand as the epitome of all victims of dominating power relations, exclusion, hegemony and systematic silencing. The constructive dimension of Jesus' messianic politics attempts here to create alternative social relations by bringing the marginalised into the centre and giving voice to the silenced ones. In our world, too, wherever this absurd logic of the last becoming the first, and the least becoming the great is practised, we see the foretaste of the reign of God.

Our discipleship journey begins from our discernment of Jesus' messianic politics. Even as we contemplate on following Jesus today, we need to ask 'what the challenges are that the metaphor of child poses before us?' A few years ago, the Indian magazine *Frontline* did a cover story on Israel's invasion of Lebanon. "Empire comes to Lebanon" was the title of that cover story.[1] That article narrates the horrific slaughter of 39 innocent children in Qana by the Israeli forces. The village where Jesus turned water into wine two thousand years ago became a small lake of blood. Conquests—whether it is political, economic, social, sexual, psychological or spiritual—continue to be the demons that possess and invade our physical bodies and our social body.

Reflecting on his exilic life, Palestinian scholar Edward Said says, "Exile is a model for the intellectuals. Even if one is not an actual immigrant, it is still possible to think as one, to imagine and investigate to move away from the centralizing authorities towards the margins." Edward Said's words are an inspiration to us on our discipleship journey in the light of Jesus' messianic politics. "A condition of marginality," he says,

> ...frees you from having always to proceed with caution, afraid to overturn the apple cart, and anxious about upsetting your colleagues. The exilic intellectual does not respond to the logic of conventional but to the audacity of daring, and to representing change, to moving on, not standing ...still.[2]

Our times are marked by stories of marginalisation, silencing, exploitation, abuse and rejection. In the Indian context, even after seven decades of independence from the shackles of colonialism, the conquest of the physical body and the social body is the everyday reality of most citizens. How are we to respond to such situations? An encounter with the face of a child is an experience of epiphany; epiphanies always challenge and invite us to take a different route on our discipleship journey. We tend to take it for granted that by virtue of our Christian identity, we are engaged in Christian discipleship. That was the mistake with Jesus' disciples too. The metaphor of child becomes paradigmatic here to understand the messianic politics and to discern the challenges of discipleship.

A few years ago, I was in the Narmada valley as part of my field research to analyse the social and environmental impact of big dams in the Narmada River. I spent a week in a village called Jalasindhi in Madhya Pradesh in central India. Jalasindhi is an Adivasi village submerged by the floodwaters from the the 138-metre Sardar Sarovar Dam on the Narmada river. Jalasindhi and neighbouring villages have no electricity, telephone, water supply, public health centres, ration shops or schools. Once a subsistence community, the people here have been displaced from their sacred abode in order to provide water and electricity to industries and elites in cities. Their story was of profound significance to my research. So, I spent a lot of time interviewing them and collecting data. I used to dream about the changes that my dissertation and my PhD would bring to my career and profile. So, I used all my time and energy to penetrate deep into their lives and gather as much data as possible for my research.

But everything turned upside down one night. We were sitting on the banks of the Narmada the day before I was to leave that village. All through my stay there, I used to ask them questions. But that evening an old woman asked me, "Son, when are you coming back?" I was shocked at that question. Why should I come back at all? I went there to do my research, and the community there was nothing but a data bank for my research. But the aged mother's question kept ringing again in my ears, "Son, when are you coming back?" It was an epiphanic moment for me. The question still haunts me.

The metaphor of the child in Jesus' discourse is an invitation to a discipleship journey. The child challenges us to look critically at our social location. The child invites us to rewrite our autobiographies.

Endnotes

[1] https://frontline.thehindu.com/cover-story/article30210545.ece

[2] Moustafa Bayoumi and Andrew Rubin, *The Edward Said Reader*, (New York: Vintage Books, 2000), 379-81.

11

Maveli: The Crucified One
John 20: 24-29

Onam is considered the national festival of the southernmost state of Kerala in India. It is a season of rejoicing and feasting, with new clothes, delicious food, family reunions, and tourist visits to what is referred to in marketing terms as "God's Own Country." Legend has it that it is the time when the virtuous *asura* king Maveli, whose throne was usurped by the jealous *devas*, makes his annual visit to see his subjects.

King Maveli's rule was a golden age where people were happy and contended. But the jealous *devas* wanted to put an end to the righteous rule of King Maveli because he was more virtuous than them. The job was given to the second person in the Vedic trinity—Vishnu, the preserver. Incarnating himself as Vamana, a dwarf, Vishnu approaches King Maveli, whose reputation for generosity was well known. Vamana impressed Maveli with his learning and then sought as a gift as much land as he could cover in three steps. Maveli granted Vamana's request. At once he turned into a giant and measured out the earth and heaven in two steps. To keep his word, Maveli offered the dwarf his head to place his promised third step; and with this Vamana pushed Maveli to Pathala, or the netherworld. But Vamana granted Maveli the right to visit his beloved land and people once a year. Thus Malayalis, the inhabitants of Kerala, observe Onam every year to welcome Maveli.

Why did the devas want to end the reign of Maveli and annihilate him? What is the reason for the rift between the devas and the asuras? According to one analyst, the asuras are shown as spiritual, divine beings in the *Rig Veda*. Etymologically, the term "*asura*" is derived from the word *asu*, meaning the "breath of God." But later, to theologically legitimise the demonisation of a race, a new etymological explanation came into being, and thus the name came to be *a-sura*, which means deprived of godliness. Thus, *asuras* came to be seen as enemies or opponents of the "gods."

Maveli represented a community in constant conflict with *devas* or a community that was destined to suffer defeats because of the machinations of *devas*. What is the significance of this story? Is it a spiritual analogy? Was Maveli a loser because he kept his word? Was his determination to keep his pledge to the dwarf an expression of his arrogant pride that deserved punishment from above? Or is the story a reassertion of the right of the dominant caste people, as representative of the gods, to grab the land of the subalterns and seize power?

In a context in which Onam has become a Brahminical ritual sponsored by the State and the Market, our attempt to rediscover the meaning of Onam has to follow a different logic; a logic that emerges from the margins. Subaltern hermeneutics is a tool that we can use as we strive to make sense of Onam from the perspectives of the descendants of Maveli.

What is subaltern hermeneutics? It is a reading strategy which appropriates and deconstructs the dominant methodologies and interpretations and consciously constructs alternative histories, narratives and spaces of empowerment. It is about listening to and 'privileging' the 'small stories' of and from the underside of history. In this short reflection, we will try to reread the Onam story alongside a biblical story and employ subaltern hermeneutics to understand them.

Onam is the remembrance of the brutal murder of an *asura* king and his dethronement by the dominant caste and class. The Lord Vishnu himself incarnates here to be the celebrant of this gruesome act of violence. The story does not end here. Some scholars say that there have been attempts to claim theological legitimacy to the act by subtly changing the king's indigenous name Maveli to 'Mahabali', which means great sacrifice. An undemocratic political coup and assassination thus becomes a virtuous and redeeming act of great sacrifice, voluntarily done by the king.

This story has parallels to the Christian story. Atonement theology is central to the Christian faith, and Sunday after Sunday we celebrate the memory of the atoning sacrifice of our Lord. What is the problem with atonement theology? It takes an act of state violence and redefines it as intimate violence, a private, spiritual transaction between God the Father and God the Son. Atonement theology says that this intimate violence saves life. This redefinition replaces state violence with intimate violence and makes intimate violence holy and salvific. Atonement theology, hence, is lethal as it legitimises terror and violence in the name of God.

A subaltern reading of the myth of Onam reveals the violence inherent in caste-ridden social relations and the way it transubstantiates violence into theological doctrines. How do Dalits and other subaltern communities make sense of this myth? Why do they still use this dominant myth of great sacrifice and celebrate Onam every year? What is the meaning of Onam for them?

Onam is a celebration of remembrance—remembrance of dangerous memories. Dangerous memories, according to Johann Baptist Metz, are "memories which make demands on us. These are memories in which earlier experiences break through to the centre-point of our lives and reveal new and dangerous insights for the present."[1] Dangerous memories are subversive memories. So, remembrance from a subaltern point of view is a political and spiritual act against all forces and systems of terror and domination. When Maveli continues to inspire Dalits and other subaltern communities to celebrate Onam "in remembrance of me," it is an invitation to be filled by these subversive memories in order to become a subversive presence in the world to "turn the world upside down."

In the Johannine narrative of the post-Easter appearance of Jesus, the Risen Lord is presented as a wounded God. Jesus appears to Thomas and other disciples as a wounded God who embodies in his body the scars of crucifixion—the impaired hands and feet, and the pierced side. Even in the most transcendent condition of physical life, the Risen Lord reveals himself as a representative of all living beings who are invaded, mutilated, silenced, crushed, abused, disabled and annihilated. Of course, the resurrection is the celebration of God's victory over death. But it is not the erasure of a long history of brutal terror and torture. Rather, it is the reenactment of the dangerous memories of all crucifixions in history which continue in different forms to this day. The Risen Lord is a wounded God.

The resurrection, as we tend to believe, is not meant to provide us with a "sense of closure," but it is a constant reminder to us to see the open wounds around us in the crucified people and the crucified earth. The dangerous memories of such victimisations enable us to locate the Risen Lord in our times.

As the Easter narratives in the Synoptic Gospels proclaim, the wounded God of Easter morning is going ahead of us to Galilee. Galilee is the borderland which in itself is an open wound and inhabited by tortured people. Here we see a radical continuity between Jesus and all victims of casteist, patriarchal, and economic violence in history. The wounded God challenges us to engage deeply with the impaired hands and the pierced sides and the crushed heads of our times. It is an invitation to embody the scars of our times. Such an engagement will initiate us into a new politics, a politics of embodiment. It is an invitation to follow the wounded God into the open wounds in our midst. It is in the open wounds of our times that we meet the Risen Lord: Maveli, the crucified one.

Endnotes

[1] Johann Baptist Metz, *Faith in History and Society: Toward a Practical Fundamental Theology*, (New York: A Crossroad Book, 1980), 109.

12

Parable of the Wicked Tenants

Matthew 21: 33-46

The five hundredth anniversary of the Reformation is an invitation to begin a new journey; a journey of thanksgiving, introspection, repentance, intercession and affirmation. It is a journey that will equip and inspire us to witness God relevantly in our times and context. The commemoration of the Reformation is not about theological nostalgia. Rather, it is about putting the Reformation into the present tense. This means not just the here and now; it means bringing the Protestant tradition and theology into the tense present—into the tensions, conflicts, violence, suffering, beauty, wonder and promise of this historical moment.

The parable of the wicked tenants begins with a situation that was common in Roman-occupied Palestine. A landowner established a vineyard, complete with a fence, a wine press, and even a watchtower. He then became an absentee landowner, returning to his own country. Tenants oversaw the vineyard and paid their rent to the owner at harvest time in the form of a share of the produce. When the owner's slaves arrived to collect his share, the tenants attacked them and even killed one of them. The owner of the vineyard then sent another delegation of slaves to collect the rent. These slaves were treated even worse than the first. Then the owner sent his son, thinking that the tenants would respect him. But the tenants killed him as well. Finally, the owner himself came, took over the vineyard from the wicked tenants and gave it to those who were committed to produce fruits.

This is a problematic text, and a difficult one to interpret on. The church interprets the parable of the wicked tenants narrated in all the Synoptic Gospels as an allegory of the murder of God's Son by the Jews and the transfer of Israel's privileges to the church. Because of this explicit tone of anti-Semitism, this passage needs to be handled with great care. Another problem with the dominant interpretation of this parable is that it removes the church from any sense of complicity in the sins mentioned in the parable and pushes them on to others. In other words, the bad guys in the parable always look like someone else and that prevents us from any kind of introspection and repentant response.

Martin Luther had to engage with problematic texts in his preaching ministry, and his advice is instructive here. According to Luther, sometimes we have to squeeze a biblical passage until it leaks the gospel. This parable is to be understood as a prophetic critique by a Jew to fellow Jews, designed not to condemn Israel but to provoke repentance. The intended message of the parable is not the demonisation of the other; rather, it is an invitation to undergo genuine introspection and repentance. So, our task is not to identify the bad guys in this story; it is rather to understand the vocation and mission of the alternative community of disciples that Jesus envisioned through this parable. The church fits the description of the wicked tenants more than the master's servants. This realisation is the starting point of reformation. The church reformed is always in need of reformation. What will the Church's repentant response look like is the question that we need to ponder on.

Coming back to the parable, Jesus has taken the old image of Israel as the vineyard under condemnation because it grew "wild grapes," (Isaiah 5: 1-7) and then he has slightly changed it. The condemnation in Jesus' retelling of the story now rests not on the nation, but on the leadership, the chief priests and the Pharisees. They are the ones who have not borne fruit. They have pretended to own the vineyard. Jesus said the vineyard would be taken away from them. But remember, it is not given to another elite group, but *to a people* who produce "the fruits of the kingdom." In other words, the church is called to produce the fruits of the reign of God in the here and now, and if we fail to do that, God's mission will continue. God will entrust the mission to those who are truly committed to be the first fruits of the reign of God.

Sola Scriptura (Scripture alone) is one of the fundamental affirmations of the church, and we claim that we are the servants of the Word. But remember, it is very easy to be the servants of the Word without disturbing the world. We have a very spiritualised and privatised understanding of the Word; a Word without any commitment to the pains, sufferings and struggles of the people; a Word that creates no problems, starts no conflicts and heals no brokenness.

The text further reminds us that Jesus is the cornerstone which breaks to pieces those who fall on it. The kingdom is taken away from those who do not bear fruit. They are crushed by the cornerstone. This text raises some important questions before us: To whose world do we belong? Are we slaves who have sold our souls to tenants who will have the kingdom of God taken away from them? Or do we welcome the son and pay our due? We cannot lead a double life. We cannot serve God and Mammon. The church is called to be a people who bear fruit. If we do not, even though we are "a church," we are on the side of the chief priests and the Pharisees.

When we identify ourselves as the tenants in the story, the first response to the text should be an honest confession of what we have done with the beautiful, abundant, liberating, inclusive good news of Jesus Christ. What implications might this parable hold for how we are producing a harvest for God's kingdom in our personal, ecclesial and public lives? What would this parable have to say to our indifference to people who are different from us? What does it have to say to our inability to forgive ourselves? Yes, we are the wicked tenants who betrayed our calling to produce the fruits of the reign of God in our neighbourhoods and communities.

The Reformation is not an epoch in history; it is a continuous experience in the life of the church. The dominant tendency is to reduce the Reformation into a past event and to idealise it uncritically. The history of Christianity, in its true sense, is the narrative and interpretation of the journey of the church engaging in the mission of bearing fruits of the reign of God. Reformation happens when the church intentionally re-forms itself to become contemporaneous and contextually relevant to engage in radical public witness. Remembrance and celebrations of the Reformation should therefore be an opportunity to keep the spirit of reformation alive in the church so that the church will continue to be a transforming and healing presence in our communities and neighbourhoods.

The parable of the wicked tenants invites us to become missional congregations. It is a call to become transformative communities, "manifesting the reign of God in their midst as lives are made new and justice is realised for those who have been denied fullness of life." Such a call challenges congregations to see mission as "the practical outworking of our faith, so that it is rooted in our communities, and grows from there engaging and transforming the challenges we face, gradually realising the fullness of life that God promises." Here we see a paradigm shift in our very understanding of mission. Mission is no longer a delegated activity that is done elsewhere, "but as part of the lifeblood of the congregation as they engage with the life experiences of their own members and the experiences of the people who comprise their neighbourhood, witnessing to their faith in God's promise of life."[1]

> A congregation cannot be missional if it is not attuned to those on the margins, either within its midst or beyond. At the heart of the Christian life there is community. This is not about institutional survival, but an expression of what our faith calls us to, the celebration of life in all its fullness, which can only be realized in community, in the company of other people. Mission is not something we can outsource, it should be the very essence of congregational life.[2]

The Reformation's anniversary is a time for genuine soul-searching for the church. Numerically speaking, Christianity is declining in the northern hemisphere. Whereas in the southern hemisphere the church is growing. Of course, we need to be worried about the numerical decline of the church in the West. But the challenge before us is more than number; the challenge is to transform the church into a transforming and healing presence in our communities. 'If your church closed its doors tomorrow, would anyone in the neighbourhood care?'

The church is facing an existential crisis in our times. It has lost its relevance. If the neighbourhood is not concerned about our existence or death, there is something terribly wrong with us. We have lost our saltiness. Rabbi Abraham Joshua Heschel's observation about the eclipse of religion is instructive here:

> It is customary to blame secular science and anti-religious philosophy for the eclipse of religion in modern society. It would be more honest to blame religion for its own defeats. Religion declined not because it was refuted, but because it became irrelevant, dull, oppressive, insipid. When faith is completely replaced by creed, worship by discipline, love by habit; when the crisis of today is ignored because of the splendour of the past; when faith becomes an heirloom rather than a living fountain; when religion speaks only in the name of authority rather than with the voice of compassion, its message becomes meaningless.[3]

African American theologian Yolanda Pierce, in the wake of Ferguson, wrote these lines:

> Even as the disciples of Jesus grieved at the foot of the cross, they understood there was work to be done. The work of justice is deeply political and requires an engagement in this present world. With tears in our eyes, we are called to march, rally, petition, sing, dance, and use whatever gifts and talents we possess for the work of justice. A grieving people need a church for such a time as this, a church that happens in their midst.[4]

Gustavo Gutierrez, in a homily preached at a Vatican gathering, challenged the church to become a Samaritan church.

> The neighbour is not the person that we find on our way, but that person that we approach to the extent we leave our own way, our own path, managing to approach others… A Samaritan church is an open church, a church attentive to human needs. We don't need a church of the pure. We need a church of the compassionate, a church known more for the people we love than the sins we condemn.[5]

How do we become a Samaritan church today? We, as a called-out community, are commissioned to bear the hope of the world in our bodies. This is the message that the parable gives us on this anniversary of the Reformation.

Endnotes

[1] Philip Woods. "CWM Perspective on Missional Congregations as Life-Affirming Communities" in *International Review of Mission*, 2014, 79.

[2] Philip Woods. "CWM Perspective on Missional Congregations as Life-Affirming Communities" in *International Review of Mission*, 2014, 79.

[3] https://sojo.net/articles/50-years-after-mlk-will-we-stand-hope

[4] https://sojo.net/articles/how-blacklivesmatter-changed-my-theology/theology-grieving-people

[5] https://www.ncronline.org/blogs/ncr-today/gutierrez-vatican-church-must-be-samaritan-reaching-out-others

13

Church reformed
is Always Being Reformed

Mark 12: 41-44

This familiar text from Mark is about what happens in the temple during Jesus' public ministry. Jesus was sitting opposite the treasury, watching the crowd put money into the treasury when a poor widow came and put in two small copper coins. Jesus brought this to the attention of his disciples and said, "This poor widow has put in more than all those who are contributing to the treasury. For all of them have contributed out of their abundance; but she out of her poverty has put in everything she had, all she had to live on" (Mark 12:44).

We use this text regularly in churches to encourage members to give generously to the church. For us, this text is all about faithful giving, sacrificial giving, and the importance of the right motives in giving. Further, the text also tends to romanticise and glorify the poor and the vulnerable for their strong faith in God and their allegiance to the church as they contribute more than the rich with the right attitude. But if we read this text in relation to the preceding and succeeding texts, we may get a new understanding of this episode and its message.

The preceding pericope (Mark 12: 38-40) narrates Jesus' criticism against the scribes and their exploitation of widows.

> Beware of the scribes, who like to walk around in long robes, and to be greeted with respect in the marketplaces, and to have the best seats in the synagogues and places of honour at banquets! They devour widows' houses and for the sake of appearance say long prayers. They will receive the greater condemnation (Mark 12: 38-40).

In both these texts Jesus contrasts the powerful with the powerless and helps us go beyond our dominant perceptions. Jesus here helps us to identify the connection between the scribes "who devour widows' houses" and the "poor widow." It is important for us to understand the meaning of this episode from the perspective of the margins. Mark 13: 1-2, the text that immediately follows this story of the poor widow, offers us more clarity on this incident. Here Jesus talks about the imminent destruction of the temple and its unjust economic and social systems and practices.

In Mark 12: 35-40, Jesus denounces the scribes and cautions the disciples and the crowd against the scribes who "devour widows' houses." While it is not quite clear what this 'devouring' means, what is clear is that in the very next verse, as Jesus watches people putting money into the treasury, there among them is "a poor widow." Jesus here is exposing the temple economy which allows the scribes to devour the houses of widows. In other words, the widow in this episode is "a poor widow" because of the unjust economic practices of the temple that "devour widows' houses."

Jesus here is not presenting the widow as a faithful giver; rather, she is presented as a victim of the oppressive practices of the scribes sanctioned by the economy and morality of the temple. This connection invites us to shift our focus from an individual (the widow) to an oppressive system (the economic practices by which the scribes devour the lives of widows). It helps us understand that this widow is not a just poor woman but an impoverished widow, impoverished by the temple, its economy, its morality, its spirituality, and its priests and officials. To put it differently, Jesus enables a deeper discernment regarding the poverty of the widow, which is the consequence of an oppressive system legitimised by religion. A sanctuary meant to enable the widow to experience freedom and life in abundance has deteriorated into a structure for social exclusion and economic exploitation.

We find similar connections in the following text as well (Mark 13: 1-2). Jesus leaves the temple and then pronounces judgment on it. While in the temple Jesus criticises the scribes; he observes the poor widow, a victim of the scribes, and finally Jesus leaves the temple and predicts its destruction. Why is Jesus angry at the temple? What is the relationship between the temple, the scribes, and the ordinary people who were "listening to Jesus with delight" as he denounced the scribes? Jesus enters the temple for the first time in Mark's Gospel in 11:11, but he does not stay long. Rather strangely, he goes to the temple, looks around, and then leaves the temple and Jerusalem, returning to Bethany. The next day he returns to Jerusalem and enters the temple again. This time Jesus acts:

> He began to drive out those who were selling and those who were buying in the temple, and he overturned the tables of the money changers and the seats of those who sold doves; and he would not allow anyone to carry anything through the temple (Mark 11: 15-16).

Having acted thus, Jesus teaches, "Is it not written, 'My house shall be called a house of prayer for all the nations?' But you have made it a den of robbers" (11:17). Immediately after this we read that

> when the chief priests and the scribes heard it [all that had happened in the temple], they kept looking for a way to kill him; for they were afraid of him, because the whole crowd was spellbound by his teaching (Mark 11:18).

Jerusalem temple is the setting in which all this action takes place. It begins with Jesus being confronted by the chief priests, the scribes and the elders as he enters the temple. Conflict with the temple leadership is a perennial theme in this unit. The literary unit further informs us of the rapport that Jesus had with the crowd. It is their support that prevents the temple authorities from acting against Jesus. Jesus then sits down opposite the temple treasury and watches people—the victims of the teaching and practices of the scribes—make their offerings. Jesus' attempt here is to demonstrate to his disciples how the temple system exploits by pointing to one of its victims, the poor widow. But the disciples are slow to understand, and they leave the temple admiring the beautiful structure. Jesus, however, does not see a beautiful building; he sees an oppressive institution that is administered by corrupt and oppressive priests and officials and he proclaims divine judgment on the temple, its economy, moralitys and religiosity. "No one stone here will be left on another; everyone will be thrown down" (Mark 13:2).

Temple criticism took centre stage in Jesus' life and ministry. He was upset with the deterioration of the place of prayer and meditation into a den of thieves. He was morally indignant at the legalism which ruled the sanctuary, denying people God's promise of healing and restoration. So, for Jesus, temple criticism was not an attempt to reject religion or religious places but an effort to reclaim the temple through radical renewal and reformation. In the history of Christianity, we see several people who have dared to invoke this Jesus tradition to transform their respective churches into what they ought to be. However, we tend to reduce the significance of the Reformation by museumising it as a historical event that happened once and for all in a particular period in history. *Ecclesia reformata, semper reformanda!* The church reformed is always being reformed!

Why do we believe that reformation has to be a continuing experience in the life of the church? Our conviction that the church must continue to be reformed comes out of our discernment of who we are. We are conscious of human fallibility and sinfulness which can deteriorate human institutions into corrupt and sinful entities. Even our best endeavours and highest aspirations are prone to sin and error. Forms of faith and life in the church are no exception here. We need to acknowledge with all humility that the church even at its best is a frail and fallible human institution. We know that we "hold these treasures in earthen vessels." Reformation is a collective act of repentance and turning back to God. Our doctrines, church constitutions and faith practices are also not infallible, and we need to submit all of them to be reformed and renewed. The church is a frail and fallible pilgrim people, a people on the way, not yet what we shall be. The church, because of who we are, remains open to always being reformed.

Our commitment to being reformed comes not only because of who we are but also because of who God is. The God "whom alone we worship and serve" is not a dead God but a living God. God is not bound to our tradition, and God the Spirit is always out of any control. No synod or ecclesiastical authority can contain, tame and domesticate the Spirit of God. God's revelation is always a surprising gift, never a given fossilised dogma or tradition. So, reformation is not only a backward movement to the Scripture, but is also a forward movement to the future of God to make us contemporaneous and contextual in our mission and witness in the world. This backward and forward reference of reform invites us on the one hand to attend respectfully to the wisdom and scriptural interpretations of those who have gone before us. On the other hand, it invites us to do more than simply reiterate what the church fathers and mothers have said and done in the past. We must be open to a radical discontinuity with the past as well. The church remains open to always being reformed.

In an address given to a youth gathering in Thiruvananthapuram in the southernmost state of Kerala in India in 1939, 23-year-old M.M. Thomas said:

> What is real Church history? It is not the history of its Popes and Archbishops. It is the history of people who, filled with the vision of a redeemed church, created strife within the church—it is the history of Luthers and Melanchthons and Abraham Malpans—of its heretics excommunicated, of its infidels martyred, for causing revolution in the church. If we are to be worthy of that heritage let us make quarrels and more quarrels within the church, for the sake of its redemption. People tell me, true and apostolic churches will never become extinct. I do not call such, Christ's church. There cannot be a true church with a continuity of existence in the world. It is a contradiction in terms. Die and

get resurrected—everyday a new fellowship—a new creation—
not the old one continuing. That alone can be Christ's church.

Ecclesia reformata, semper reformanda!

Endnotes

[1] M.M. Thomas, *Ideological Question Within Christian Commitment*, (Bangalore: CLS/CISRS, 1983), 31.

14

Lent: Church Happening at the Margins

Mark 1: 40-45

Lent, for most of us, is primarily a season of disengagement, staying away from the temptations of the material world. It is a season of abstinence. Our Lenten observations propagate a spirituality that rejects materiality. But this text does not endorse this understanding of a disengaged spirituality. Rather, it invites us to have a radical engagement in the material world. The text witnesses to the presence of Jesus in the life stories of outcasts, proclaiming them as heirs of salvation. We meet the divine in this text as a therapeutic presence enabling the outcasts to experience healing and fullness of life.

Lent is an invitation to make courageous choices to bring about healing and restoration

In this episode, we see a leprosy patient approaching Jesus for healing and restoration. His request to Jesus is quite interesting. "If you choose, you can make me clean" (Mark 1:40). The man did not ask Jesus to heal him. He asked Jesus to make him clean. Why did he insist that Jesus cleanse him? In the Jewish tradition, leprosy was considered a dreaded disease that made the person ritually unclean. The idea of purity in Jewish religiosity and ethics had classifications such as sacred places and defiled places, sacred time and impure time or period, and pure person and polluted person. We see this in all religious traditions. The controversy around allowing women of menstruating age to enter the Sabarimala temple in Kerala, India, is an example of such purity maps. In the Jewish tradition, it is the purity map that determined one's space in the religious and social order. An "unclean" or "impure" person thus classified was ostracised by the community. Leprosy patients were outcasts in biblical times, for whom the social exclusion and stigma were more painful and humiliating than the sickness. The man in this story asked Jesus to make him clean so that he can be part of the community and live life with dignity.

According to the laws of purity in the book of Leviticus, a practising Jew should not have any contact with a leprosy-affected person (Leviticus 13). It is in this context that we need to revisit the man's request to Jesus, "If you choose, you can make me heal." He knew that Jesus would not be comfortable in engaging with a leper. But still he decided to encounter Jesus and challenge him to make a choice. "If you choose, you can make me heal." Jesus had two options: one, to ignore the man and his plea and follow the moral and religious codes of his religion and community, or two, to disrupt the moral codes of his religion and help an outcast to experience healing and dignity. This episode is the story of a leprosy-affected person, an outcast, helping Jesus to discern his vocation. And Jesus responded, "Brother, I do choose, be made clean!" (Mark 1:41).

Lent is a time for vocational discernment rather than giving up something. It is a time to critically evaluate our attitude towards people who are marginalised because of unjust religious and moral codes. Lent is a time to make courageous choices in our lives to help others flourish in their lives. If we continue to consider Lent as a season of disengagement, we can remain in our comfort zones and sanctuaries without responding to the pain and pathos of our brothers and sisters who long for healing and human dignity. But if we consider Lent as a season of radical engagement, God will empower us to make choices that will make a difference in the life of others. If we choose, we can make a difference.

Lent is an invitation to touch the untouchables

According to Leviticus 5:3, touching a leprosy-affected person can make a person unclean and ritually impure. This further entails barring entry to the temple and excommunication from society. When the man requested Jesus to make him clean, Jesus realised that it was not his sickness but the sinful religious practices of the Jewish community that had made him an outcast. Jesus had to handle this with discernment. He already knew that the infected body of the man required healing. But the new discernment enabled Jesus to realise that more than the leprosy-affected person, it is his community that needed healing. Healing from the sinful notions of purity and pollution that demonise and stigmatise people. Such wholistic healing required the nerve to disrupt Jewish religiosity and morality and Jesus showed the courage to do that. "Moved with pity, Jesus stretched out his hand and touched him, and said to him, 'I do choose. Be made clean!' Immediately the leprosy left him, and he was made clean." Jesus was moved with pity. The root word for pity also means anger. Yes, Jesus was moved with anger at the sinful system that dehumanised the man.

Lent is an invitation to touch the untouchables. Jesus could have healed the man with a word; he did not need to touch him. According to the Jewish tradition, Jesus became an outcast by touching the untouchable. With this audacious act, Jesus replaced the inhuman religiosity and morality with the inclusive gospel of the kingdom of God. This episode tells us that Jesus was not interested in treating the symptom but in striking at the root of the problem.

If we consider Lent as a season of disengagement, we do not have to be worried about the unjust laws and practices prevalent in our society. But Lent is a season of engagement. Filled by the spirit of Christ, we are called to touch the untouchables. Lent is a season to reclaim that tradition and to make a difference in the lives of people who are pushed to the peripheries. For that we need to be moved by pity. We need to be angry at the systems that marginalise and dehumanise people who are created in the image of God. If we allow ourselves to be moved by compassion and rightful indignation, we will become a healing presence in communities.

Lent is an invitation to make the church an inclusive community

After the man was healed, Jesus said to him, "Go, show yourself to the priest, and offer for your cleansing what Moses commanded, as a testimony to them" (Mark 1:44). Healing is incomplete without restoration in the community. According to the Jewish law, priests had to certify the healing that had happened to a leprosy patient. Healing and curing are two different things. For Jesus, healing included both physical curing and restoration in the community. Unfortunately, we have the tendency to discriminate and stigmatise people based on their health conditions. A church that closes its door to the outcasts and the marginalised is not the church of Christ.

Discrimination is antithetical to the calling of the church. The church should become a welcoming space for all God's children, irrespective of their caste, race, ethnicity, economic status, sexual orientation and health condition. We should be able to come to the house of God just as we are. There are no preconditions to become the children of God. The assurance of the grace of God is sufficient for us to come to the throne of grace. The church is called to be a rainbow community. A church that practices untouchability is a church that needs healing. When the leprosy-affected person was restored back to the fellowship of the faith community, the faith community was also healed.

Lent is not just a season for individual penitence and repentance. Lent is also a time for penitence, repentance, and transformation of the church. It is a time for us to engage in genuine introspection and to see how we continue to alienate and marginalise people from our fellowship. We need to critically evaluate whether our ministries, practices and rules and regulations are stumbling blocks for people to experience fellowship and healing. We need to commit to transform our church into a sanctuary where people feel welcomed, loved, healed and empowered.

Lent offers us the opportunity to meet Jesus at the margins. He is calling us to follow him to the margins and become a healing presence in the lives of the outcasts. Lent is a call to radical engagement. It is a call to make a choice in our lives; a choice to come out of our comfort zones and to make a difference in the lives of others. Lent is also a call to touch the untouchables. A touch, a smile or a hug is therapeutic. It is contagious. It can spread healing and restoration in our communities. Our Lenten engagement at the margins helps us to rediscover the church. The church will happen as a sanctuary of love, acceptance, fellowship, and healing in the streets. Instead of giving up something during Lenten season, let us engage ourselves in the lives of those who are longing for healing and dignity.

15

For Such a Time as This: Living out the Easter Faith

Mark 16: 1-20

The resurrection is a foundational doctrinal affirmation of the church. But what does it mean to us? How do we become an Easter community and live out the Easter faith in the here and now? As theologian Marcus Borg reminds us,

> You won't find Jesus in the land of the dead. He is still with us. The powers killed him — but they couldn't stop him. They crucified him and buried him in a rich man's tomb. But imperial execution and a tomb couldn't hold him. He's still loose in the world. He's still out there, still here, still recruiting people to share his passion for the Kingdom of God — a transformed world here and now. It's not over.

This means Jesus is resurrected into our everyday experiences. From a speculative dogma, the resurrection becomes a living experience in the world when the church transforms itself into an Easter community.

The gospel of Mark is the first and the most authentic gospel in the New Testament. However, it is interesting that Mark's

Gospel ends rather abruptly. The earlier manuscripts of Mark's Gospel end at verse 8 of chapter 16. What we have today is a longer ending (9-20) which is considered an addition to the original text. Mark 16: 1-8 narrates the story of the Galilean women's journey on that Sunday morning to the tomb of our Lord. As the Gospel accounts testify, these women were with Jesus when he was crucified and buried. Even as they walked towards the tomb on that Sunday morning, they were confronted with a huge problem, "Who will roll away the stone for us?"

The sealed tomb represented the demise of their hope. The stone at the entrance of the tomb marked the end of their long friendship and fellowship with Jesus, their master and friend. It is this very same stone that compelled Peter and his friends to return to the safety and security of their old profession of fishing. The stone at the tomb sealed by the religious and political authorities of the time was a symbolic message to Jesus' friends and followers: Your Lord is no more in control. The sealed tomb was the declaration of a regime change. It was the massacre of the dreams and visions of the Galilean multitudes that followed Jesus.

Who will roll away the stone is a question that confronts us every day. A sealed tomb is the symbol of shattered hopes. It is the ultimate experience of utter God-forsakenness. Our dreams and our hopes are buried in this valley of despair. We live with the tragic reality of sealed tombs in our midst. We see around us cemeteries of hope sealed with boulders. In the valley of sealed tombs, our ability to dream and hope simply dies. The place of hope is occupied by despair. Like the Galilean women, we, too, in a feeble voice lament, "Who will roll away these stones for us?" (Mark 16:3).

The resurrection story in Mark does not end with the stone being removed from the entrance of the tomb. Rather, it invites us to introspect and reflect on our understanding of God and our Christian discipleship. The Markan writer here rejects two dominant God concepts which we all share—the 'entombed' God and the 'enthroned' God. An entombed God is central to our own religiosity. It is always comfortable to worship and follow a deceased God. Remembering his passion and death, singing praises to him, and recalling his mighty deeds occupy the central part of our religious life. An entombed God is a domesticated God. He is a harmless God who never intervenes in our affairs, nor disturbs our projects and interests. We visit the entombed God once a week to pay our homage to him. For the remaining six days, he will be in his tomb and we continue with our business as usual. We pray earnestly to roll away the stones that kill our hope in life. But we are comfortable with an entombed God so that we can remain in our comfort zones and claim that we are his people.

The enthroned God is yet another popular and dominant understanding of God where our faith is in a God who is enthroned in heaven, aloof from worldly realities. It is a triumphalist model that reduces the significance of the cross in the salvific action of God in history. This God concept can be easily manipulated to legitimise our vested interests. The commonality in both these models is the total absence of the organic presence of the living God in history. As a result, spirituality is understood as paying homage to a deceased or trans-historical God who is not concerned about the way we live out our faith. The theology of Jesus entombed and enthroned is the theology that the church is most interested in. As a result, we prefer a confessional orthodoxy over costly practices of discipleship. We are more interested in building monuments and maintaining them than becoming radical movements of disciples. Our aspiration is to get into positions of control and power and live in awe and wonder of the architecture of domination than of servanthood.

Having realised the perversions of our doctrines and religiosity, what should be a relevant Easter message for us? Do we find an alternative in Mark's abruptly ended story? Mark begins his Gospel with the good news of Jesus Christ who appears in Galilee with his message of repentance and discipleship. Mark ends his Gospel with the proclamation that "He has been raised; he is not here. But, go tell his disciples and Peter that he is going ahead of you to Galilee; there you will see him, just as he told you" (Mark 16: 6-8). The resurrection is the embodiment of the divine in the lives and struggles of the multitudes in today's Galilees.

Mark's Gospel is known as the story of discipleship. Mark's story ends as it began, inviting us to follow Jesus. The message of Mark's Easter story is a call to discipleship; to follow the Risen Lord to the Galilees of our times. Yes, Mark's Gospel ends abruptly. It ends abruptly because it believes in the potential of the disciples to become the gospel as they live out their faith in today's Galilees. It is by following the crucified Christ that we witness the risen Christ in our times. Mark's Easter story provides us with the lens to discern the social location of the risen Lord so that we can be his witnesses there.

In the midst of hopelessness, the Galilean women saw a ray of hope. As Mark narrates, "When they looked up, they saw that the stone which was very large had already been rolled back" (Mark 16:4). The good news of Easter is the very assurance that even when we live amid death, we are surrounded by the promise that death does not have the final say over us. Easter is the resurrection of hope from the cemetery of despair. As the mythical phoenix, hope resurrects from the ashes of tragedy. It is the assurance that because Jesus lives there is hope for tomorrow. When the Galilean women who were lamenting "Who will roll away the stone for us" looked up, they experienced Easter. 'Looking up' is the verb that Mark uses to describe how the blind men regained their sight. It is Mark's metaphor for a faith that looks more deeply into what appears to be, to see what really is. It means to re-vision. It means to reclaim the promise of God to be God's Easter presence in our communities as we engage in the mission of rolling away the stones that seal hope.

The message of Easter is to stop looking for messiahs who will roll away the stones for us. Instead, Easter invites us to look up and re-vision so that our moral agency to roll away the stones will be enabled. This is the mountain-moving faith that Jesus instilled in us. We need to have the audacity of faith to believe that we can move mountains and we can roll away the stones. We become an Easter community when we look up and discern different communities and movements at the margins, engaging in the mission of removing the stones. It is through our organic solidarity with such movements that we become an Easter community, living out the Easter faith.

Unfortunately, instead of becoming an Easter community, we prefer to remain as boulders that enslave life and hope. When we profess that Jesus' vision of the kingdom of God was and is, for all practical purposes, a well-meaning delusion, we become stones that prevent people from dreaming and envisioning alternatives. When we use power to rule over others, to shame and humiliate people who disagree with us, to demonise and discriminate people who are different from us, we reinforce the boulders to suffocate hope. When we abstain ourselves from witnessing God in the public sphere through our ministries of resistance, nonconformism, care and compassionate justice because of our fear of the state, we cease to be an Easter community. We have distorted the Gospel story so as to make it conform to the ethos of the prevailing order so that our institutional interests and personal ambitions are protected.

Easter visits us every year with a renewed call to follow Jesus who has gone ahead of us to Galilee. It is a call to discipleship. It is a call to constantly examine our desire to become citizens of Jerusalem. Easter is also a time to evaluate our priorities in life—personal, ecclesial and institutional lives. Easter is a call for a radical social relocation, to be a sojourner with Jesus and give hope and life to those who live in despair and hopelessness by being part of the divine mission of rolling the stones away.

"Why do you search for the living among the dead? He is not here. He is going before you to Galilee; there you will see him." Jesus goes ahead of the church, Jesus goes ahead of our theological institutions, proclaiming liberation from our Christologies of entombment and enthronement, to spearhead a system-threatening movement of the multitudes in the Galilees of our times.

Following Jesus to the Galilees of our times can be as dangerous and risky as cutting the branch on which we are comfortably settled. The message of Easter is absurd. It demands from us a costly commitment. When we become a mountain-moving community, the world will experience the power of resurrection in and through us. For such a time as this, we are called to be an Easter community, living out the Easter faith. Christ is Risen. Indeed, he is Risen. Alleluia!

Endnotes

[1] https://marcusjborg.org/reflections-on-easter/

16

Let my People Go so that they may (not) Worship the (un)god!

Exodus 32

When Yahweh commissioned Moses to lead the liberation struggle of the enslaved people in Egypt, Yahweh instructed Moses to go to Pharaoh and tell him: "Let my people go so that they may worship me." In our dominant interpretations, we tend to think that God liberated the enslaved people because in Egypt they did not have the freedom to worship the true God. In other words, it means it was not the sinfulness of slavery that prompted God to initiate their freedom from Egypt but the specific purpose of worshipping God. A careful reading of the book of Exodus will throw light on the fact that the people were worshipping God regularly while they were still slaves in Egypt. Even during their liberation struggle they were involved in elaborate observations of religious feasts and rituals, affirming publicly their faith in Yahweh. Also, it is interesting to note that the Bible does not indicate that there was a qualitative difference in the worship life of the liberated slaves in the wilderness. How do we theologically understand the connection between liberation from the shackles of oppression and worship? What is the meaning of worship in the context of new Pharaohs who demand our allegiance and claim lordship over us?

Prayer, according to Jewish theologian Rabbi Abraham Joshua Heschel, "is meaningless unless it is subversive, unless it seeks to overthrow and to ruin the pyramids of callousness, hatred, opportunism, and falsehoods."[1] To put it differently, worship is a subversive activity that contests and overthrows the prevailing sinful order of injustice and inequality. For Moses, the Mount Horeb experience was not only an alternative experience of theophany but also a tutorial for an alternative understanding of worship. The alternative experience of theophany enabled Moses to reimagine God as the vulnerable One, deeply affected by the scars of slavery. In the vision of the burning bush, Moses encountered God as a co-sufferer who was embodied in the life stories of pain, pathos, and struggles for freedom and dignity of the enslaved communities. The sacramental and liturgical symbol of fire in the burning bush provided Moses with an alternative understanding of worship. Worship ought to instill in the enslaved community the audacity to believe that the blazing fire of the empire cannot destroy the beauty of life. The green leaves in the liturgy of the burning bush empowered Moses to believe in the possibility of a beyond of Egypt.

Moses' commissioning into the mission of liberation was also a liturgical act. He was asked to remove his sandals because he was standing on sacred ground. We can also interpret Moses' removing of sandals as a rite of passage or an initiation ritual to be enfleshed in the struggles of the colonised people. In fact, it was a public denouncement of his privileges and power which was a prerequisite to get organically connected with and grounded in the struggles of the underdogs. Worship is therefore a life-changing experience where we are invited to realise and denounce our power and privileges in order to become credible and authentic comrades of the communities at the margins who are engaged in the salvific mission of turning the world upside down.

"Let my people go so that they may worship me" does not mean that God's liberative mission is to enable us to worship God in a safe and comfortable space; rather the very struggle for liberation is an act of worship. Let us paraphrase Rabbi Heschel's interpretation of prayer contextually. Worship is our political engagement to overthrow and ruin the pyramids of economic injustice, and social exclusion such as casteism, patriarchy, and heterosexism. Such discernment helps us to go beyond our binary thinking of worship and community work, and ministry and social action.

God liberated the slaves from their bondage in Egypt. But they ended up creating and worshipping idols. The story of the golden calf is an invitation to critically evaluate our faith and spirituality to see whether we have replaced the God of the oppressed with the ungods of power, prosperity and status quo. All human initiatives of liberation in history unfortunately have the potential to become oppressive, thanks to the reality of sin and our inability for self-redemption. When we absolutise our fragmentary liberation experiences as ultimate victories, we fail to recognise the pervading hegemonic presence of the empire within us which lure us into internalising and embracing the logic and culture of the very pyramids that we destroyed in our liberation struggles. The story of the golden calf reminds us that the betrayal of our liturgical celebration of liberation is theologically legitimised through the liturgy of the ungods.

The liberated slaves in their journey towards the Promised Land experienced Yahweh as the journeying God. But when Moses, who went up the mountain to receive the commandments, delayed his return even after forty days and nights, the people became anxious and proposed that Aaron "make gods for us, who shall go before us." What we find here is the human tendency to reduce the mystery called the divine into idols of certainty. We also see here the institutionalisation of a faith movement for liberation into an organised religion with its hierarchy, priesthood, rules and regulations, and the apparatus and paraphernalia of spirituality.

The dominant always uses religious institutions and religious leaders to exploit the religious sentiments of the common people to grab their possessions to create new idols that ensure them prosperity and power. This was precisely the role of Aaron in this story. Idolatry is nothing but the fetishisation of our imperial projects, and liturgy in the context of idolatry celebrates the sacrifice of the powerless and the voiceless at the altar of patriotism, progress, family values and cultural nationalism. The history of Christianity is also the history of the creation of golden calves. Ungods are created in history to offer spiritual and theological legitimisation to the pyramids of injustice and exclusion.

For Sebastian Kappen, the Christian Ungod

> is the god whom Christians fashioned to legitimize their lust for wealth and power. It is the Christian ungod who authorized the Christian kings to colonize and enslave all pagan nations and to exterminate indigenous tribes of the Americas and Australia. It is the Christian ungod who permitted the Trans-Atlantic slave trade involving more than 30 million Africans. In short, the Christian ungod is a god who takes the side of the affluent and

powerful against the vulnerable, a god with hands dripping with the blood of the innocent.[2]

The history of Christianity in India is also not different. At critical times in the country's history, we have betrayed our faith in God and worshipped the ungod. Patriotism, progress, development, caste privilege, patriarchy, heteronormativity, regionalism…the list of golden calves continues. Many a time we become worshippers of the ungods to protect and safeguard vested interests. We are more comfortable in depending on the mercy of the ungods who rule us than in the empowering presence of the liberating God. We have lost the courage of the early church to say boldly, "We must obey God rather than any human authority."

Today, in the context of fascism making its entry, we have betrayed our calling and become followers of the golden calves. Here we are surrounded by a cloud of witnesses and we need to listen to their voices. When the German churches legitimised the fascist tyranny of the Nazi regime, the Confessing Church came out with the *Barmen Declaration* affirming that,

> We reject the false doctrine that the Church could have permission to hand over the form of its message and of its order to whatever it itself might wish or to the vicissitudes of the prevailing ideological and political convictions of the day.[3]

The *Kairos Document* from South Africa reminds us that,

> State theology is simply the theological justification of the status quo with its racism, capitalism and totalitarianism. It blesses injustice, canonizes the will of the powerful and reduces the poor to passivity, obedience and apathy.[4]

Four decades ago, when India encountered fascism in the form of the 'Emergency', churches and ecumenical movements in general were competing to worship the ungod. But there was a remnant within the remnant, and they had the audacity to challenge and dismantle the golden calf. The National Council of Churches in India's (NCCI) campaign "no one can serve Christ and caste" is yet another attempt to denounce the legitimacy of the golden calves.

If we read the gospel narrative of the widow's mite (Mark 12: 41-44) juxtaposed with the story of the golden calf, we see a lot of parallels. We see the way religion legitimises oppressive systems and unjust structures, which are antithetical to the gospel message. Religion, with its distorted theology, liturgy and morality continues to incorporate its followers into a band of idol worshippers. We have lost our ability to distinguish between the God of life and the ungods of prosperity and power. We have become devotees of the golden calves.

In our times it has become not just illegitimate to speak against the golden calves, it can also cost our lives and jobs. This challenges us to continue the exodus even in the Promised Land. Egypt is around us and within us, and we need to discern it and gather the prophetic courage to destroy the golden calves of our times. It is our faith imperative to occupy our churches, our spiritual practices and our institutions to reclaim them from the worship of the ungods. It is in our unending journey towards freedom, dismantling the pyramids of systemic sin and evil, that we worship the God of life in truth and spirit. Let my people go so that they may not worship the ungods.

Endnotes

[1] Rabbi Abraham Joshua Heschel. Quoted in "On Prayer," in *Moral Grandeur and Spiritual Audacity*, Susannah Heschel, ed. (New York: Farrar Straus Giroux, 1996), 257.

[2] Sabastian Kappen. *Spirituality in the Age of Recolonization*. (Bangalore: Visthar, 1995), 3.

[3] https://www.spucc.org/sites/default/files/BARMEN%20DECLARATION%20UCC.pdf

[4] https://kairossouthernafrica.wordpress.com/2011/05/08/the-south-africa-kairos-document-1985/

17

Faith in the Context
of God-forsakenness

Habakkuk 1: 1-4, 2: 1-4

This is a text that talks about faith in the context of utter God-forsakenness. Habakkuk was confronted with the question of evil. Why is God allowing the righteous to suffer and die unjustly? Why is injustice not punished? In the language of theology, we call it theodicy or the problem of evil. If God is good and omnipotent, how is it that evil exists? Should we believe that the events in our lives include divinely ordained punishments and divinely ordered rewards? The challenge of believing in the ultimate power of justice in a world that appears to be overwhelmingly unjust is the most difficult existential struggle for us.

The literary format of the book of Habakkuk is that of a psalm of lament. The prophet is a worshipper in distress who appeals for divine intervention. The lament is also a complaint; it is a complaint against the lack of justice in Judean society and God's failure to act against it. The prophet then explains the problem. "Destruction and violence are before me; strife and contention arise. So, the law becomes slack and justice never prevails. The wicked surround the righteous, therefore judgement comes forth perverted" (Hab 1:3-4). The description of injustice presented by the prophet here may appear to be too general. So, it is important for us to identify the real problem. Scholars suggest different possibilities. It could be the oppression of Judea by the Assyrian Empire. It could also be the abuse of power by King Jehoiakim of Judea. Violence and destruction may be owing to the ruthless accumulation of wealth by the rich and the ruling class. There is also a criticism of the judicial system in Judea which perverted justice. Freedom of expression was also curtailed.

The books of Jeremiah and II Kings provide us a picture of the brutal regime of King Jehoiakim. He used forced and unpaid labour for building his palaces. He also demanded heavy payments from citizens to support his alliances with Egypt and other countries. Jehoiakim was notorious for his obstruction of justice, shedding of innocent blood, and the killing of prophets. It is in this context that Habakkuk cries aloud on behalf of the victims who he calls the 'righteous'.

The uniqueness of the book of Habakkuk is its attempt to problematise divine justice. Habakkuk's lament is not just a judgment oracle; it is an argument with God. "O Lord, how long shall I cry for help and you will not listen? Or cry to you of violence and you will not save?" (Hab 1:2). Arguing with God in the face of injustice is a tradition that we see in the Hebrew Bible. There is a story of a certain Jew who prayed for a specific result and when God failed to answer the prayer, the Jew stopped asking for that thing from God. When the Jew died, he met God and asked, "Why didn't you answer my prayer?" God replied, "Because you did not protest long enough."

When the Malayalam title of M.M. Thomas' commentary on the book of Job is translated, it reads, "Faith that is strengthened through questioning God." For Thomas, protest atheism is central to an authentic faith in God. Habakkuk provides us with a new perspective on arguing with God. When the experience of the victims becomes the locus of our faith, we discern in our everyday life discrepancies between the experience of the victims and the ideals and visions of our faith. There we begin to argue with God and even question God. When Habakkuk is confronted with the discrepancies between faith in a just God and the experience of an unjust world, God comes across as being either uninterested or unable to do justice.

When injustice shadows the vision of the reign of God, it is easy to hope for heaven and relinquish the world. Another means of escapism, which we all practice, is to get into the consolation mood by proclaiming, 'God knows best.' But Habakkuk begs to differ from us. He believed in the possibility of a beyond of the present, and persistently asks God, "Why are you silent when the wicked swallow up the righteous?" (Hab 1:13). The protest atheism that we find in the Hebrew religion is inspired by the faith in the God of justice and God's promises. So, Habakkuk's questioning of God comes out of a faithful commitment to God's justice even when such justice appears to be absent in the world.

After raising these questions, Habakkuk waits patiently for God's answer, as narrated in chapter 2:1: "I will stand at my watchpost, and station myself on the rampart; I will keep watch to see what he will say to me." This indicates the prophet's commitment to establish God's justice on earth. When our faith is formulated in the everyday living experiences of the wretched of the earth, we develop the revolutionary patience to wait for the realisation of that new heaven and new earth. Then God assures him, "There is still a vision for the appointed time. It will surely come. It will not delay. The righteous shall live by their faith" (Hab 2:3).

Faith in God is a faith in God's promises to restore the face of the earth. This restoration or the realisation of the reign of God is an existential need for the victims who Habakkuk calls the 'righteous'. The faith of the victims in a God that is faithful to God's promises strengthens us as we confront the theodicy question in our times. The righteous shall live by faith.

Luke the Evangelist narrates a conversation between Jesus and his disciples where the disciples ask Jesus to increase their faith. But Jesus replies, "If you have faith as a grain of mustard seed, you could say to this sycamore tree, 'Be uprooted and planted in the sea,' and it would obey you" (Luke 17: 5-6). A sycamore tree is a large tree with deep roots and grows up to 60 feet. The parallels of this text in Matthew and Mark talk about mountain-moving faith. So, Jesus juxtaposes here a mustard seed and a sycamore tree to convince the disciples of the power of faith to move mountains. The conversation started with a request from the disciples to increase their faith. But Jesus' diagnosis is different. For him, what they needed was not more faith, but a different understanding of faith. Then he explained the foolish logic of a faith that believes in the possibility of a mustard seed moving mountains.

Jesus uses the metaphor of the mustard seed to articulate the logic of the reign of God.

> With what can we compare the kingdom of God? It is like a mustard seed, which, when sown upon the ground, is the smallest of all seeds on earth, yet when it is sown it grows up and becomes the greatest of all shrubs, and puts forth large branches, so that

the birds of the air can make nests in its shade (Mark 4.30).

Those who are familiar with mustard plants know that this is a silly example. But that is the mystery of faith. When the vulnerable, the weak and the underdogs assume historical agency, even mountains are in trouble. This is the absurd logic of Christian faith. Mustard seeds moving mountains. Davids defeating Goliaths. Communities of faith turning the world upside down. So, Jesus' prescription for the disciples was not to strive for more faith in a quantitative sense; rather, it is to grasp the absurd logic of faith and be possessed by it. The righteous shall live by faith.

The problem of evil, therefore, is a question of our faith. When our faith is moulded in the everyday living experiences of the victims of our times, when we persistently argue with God in the face of injustice, our faith becomes little mustard seeds that can move mountains. Our context is not much different from that of Habakkuk. We are surrounded with mountains and sycamore trees. We have lost our faith in a world beyond the present, and we are seeking comfort zones in this world of injustice.

June Jordan, an African American poet, writes, "We are the ones we've been waiting for."[1] As Alice Walker observes,

> we are the ones we've been waiting for because we are able to see what is happening with a much greater awareness than our parents or grandparents could see. Having seen the greater truth of the pervasiveness of injustice around us, we do not want to believe that we can "fix" things.[2]

But when we become baptised in this new faith we do not want to believe that the mountains are there forever. We do not want the perpetuation of an economic order which causes the rich to become ever more callous and complacent and the poor to become ever more wretched and humiliated. We are not willing to ignore starving and brutalised children. We will not let women be stoned or abused without protest. We refuse to stand quietly by as farmers are destroyed by people who have never farmed, and plants are engineered to self-destruct. We will not remain as passive and loyal church members as long as the church continues to legitimise the powers that be. We are the ones we've been waiting for.

Many people in our world have already inherited this faith and affirm that we are the ones we have been waiting for. They are the ones who go to places like Iraq and Gaza and place their bodies between the bombs of the United States and Israel and the infrastructure of the local water supply. They are the ones who collect food and medicine for those deprived. They are the university students who fill jails in India singing songs of *azadi*, freedom and democracy. They are the ones, who have been under detention for months in Kashmir in the name of national security. Like Habakkuk, they are disturbed by the discrepancies between their faith in a just world and the reality of the sway of evil and injustice. They are not interested in discussing the problem of evil metaphysically. Rather, as inheritors of this new faith they believe that they are the ones they have been waiting for. The righteous shall live by faith.

In his Letter from Birmingham Jail, addressing the white clergy who challenged his struggle for racial justice, Dr. Martin Luther King Jr. said,

> If today's church does not recapture the sacrificial spirit of the early church, it will lose its authenticity, forfeit the loyalty of millions, and be dismissed as an irrelevant social club with no meaning for the twentieth century.[3]

Dr. King's critique applies to us as well. Why are we here? What are we doing here? How are we equipping ourselves? As Michel Foucault reminds us,

> The work of an intellectual is not to shape others' political will; it is, through the analysis that he carries out in his own field, to question over and over again what is postulated as self-evident, to disturb people's mental habits, the way they do and think things, to dissipate what is familiar and accepted, to reexamine rules and institutions and on the basis of this re-problematization,… to participate in the formation of a political will.[4]

The righteous shall live by faith. We are the ones we've been waiting for.

Endnotes

[1] http://www.junejordan.net/poem-for-south-african-women.html

[2] https://www.feminist.com/resources/artspeech/genwom/wearetheones.html

[3] https://www.africa.upenn.edu/Articles_Gen/Letter_Birmingham.html

[4] Michael Foucault. "The Concern for Truth". In L. D. Kritzman (Ed.) *Michel Foucault: Politics, philosophy, culture. Interviews and other writings, 1977-1984*, (New York: Routledge, 1988), 265.

18

"We must obey God rather than any human authority"

Acts 5: 27-42

The Pentecost event made the early church a spirit-filled church. Disappointed by the untimely death of their master, the disciples were negotiating their return to their old professions. But the Pentecost transformed everything. Return to normalcy is not an option for a spirit-filled person and community. On the day of Pentecost we see ecclesio-genesis, the birthing of the church. The Acts of the Apostles narrate how the church happened as a community that preaches the gospel of the redemption of Jesus Christ and manifests the partial realisation of that redemption in their community through sharing, caring, healing and restoration.

Pentecost, the coming of the Holy Spirit, did not help the disciples and the faith community to solve their problems; rather it created new problems. The preaching and the acts of healing by Peter and John resulted in their arrest. The "signs and wonders" that the apostles performed led to their arrest again. The text narrates their third arrest and the trial before the religious court, the Sanhedrin, for violating the strict orders "not to teach in the name of Jesus." In the courtroom, when they were questioned by scholarly men, Peter, "the ordinary and uneducated man," was very categorical in his response: "We must obey God rather than any human authority." The gospel of Christ, which they believed with all their heart, is something they felt compelled to share in order that others might experience the new life. The Pentecost event changed their lives, empowering them to preach, teach and heal in the name of Jesus. Whenever the early Christians entered a town, the people in power were disturbed and immediately sought to convict the Christians for being "disturbers of the peace." But the Christians pressed on in the conviction that they were called to obey God rather than human beings. Though small in number, they were big in commitment.

Christian life is in constant tension between the demands of the temporal authorities and the demands of Christian discipleship. In such contexts civil disobedience becomes a Christian imperative for us to be authentic in our Christian discipleship and witnessing. How do we define civil disobedience? Civil disobedience is purposeful, nonviolent action, or refusal to act, by a Christian who believes such action or inaction is required of him or her in order to be faithful to God, and which s/he knows will be treated by the authorities as a violation of law.

There are times when the law of the nation, the rules and regulations of the church and its institutions, and the expectations of the society and the family are contrary to the will of God. Are we ethically obliged to obey those rules, laws and expectations, which according to our conscience, are against God's righteousness? We too have had our courtroom experiences where we have shared Peter's agony of confronting the Sanhedrin. We will face several such experiences in the future as well. But do we have the audacity of faith to categorically affirm that "we must obey God rather than any human authority?"

As we continue to wrestle with the ethical rightness of civil disobedience, we are surrounded by a cloud of witnesses in the Bible who can inspire and inform us in our ethical discernment. Shiphrah and Puah, the Hebrew midwives, disobeyed the order by Pharaoh to do what is right in obedience to God. Prophet Samuel initiated a political coup by anointing David as king while Saul was still reigning as king. We see this spirit of righteousness and nonconformism in Queen Vasthi when she disobeyed the instructions of the king. In the book of Daniel, we see the courage of a few young men who refused to bow down and worship the king's golden image. Jesus, forever a nonconformist, always placed human beings above rules and traditions and violated rules and laws to demonstrate the compassionate justice and the inclusivity of the reign of God.

We are also surrounded by a cloud of witnesses in our own history who have showed the courage to continue this apostolic praxis of Christian disobedience and nonconformism. At the Diet of Worms, which included both civil and ecclesiastical authorities, Martin Luther stated,

> Unless I am convicted by Scripture and plain reason—I do not accept the authority of popes and councils, for they have contradicted each other. My conscience is captive to the word of God. I cannot and I will not recant anything, for to go against conscience is neither right nor safe.[1]

Mahatma Gandhi believed that "civil disobedience becomes a sacred duty when the state has become lawless or corrupt. And a citizen who barters with such a state shares in its corruption and lawlessness."[2] For Martin Luther King Jr., "An individual who breaks a law that conscience tells him is unjust, and who willingly accepts the penalty of imprisonment in order to arouse the conscience of the community over its injustice, is in reality expressing the highest respect for the law."[3]

When the Indian Christian community slavishly supported the unjust regime of Indira Gandhi during the political emergency in India, a remnant within the Indian Christian community showed the courage to say no to the powers that be. Today, we live in a context of fascism and state totalitarianism. What is the witness of the Indian church today? When fascist forces try to divide the country and destroy the secular fabric of our nation, how can we remain silent? We betray our calling when we become silent in the face of fascism. Today we see the celebration of the apostolic tradition of nonconformism and civil disobedience in our streets, universities and jails where spirit-filled students, young people, women and minorities resist the fascist ideology of exclusion. We see the genesis of a new *ekklesia* in these communities of resistance and reconstruction. How do we become a church today? Samuel Rayan's poem is instructive here. "A candlelight is a protest at midnight. It is a non-conformist. It says to the darkness, I beg to differ."[4] This is the vocation of the church in India today, and we see church happening in the Shaheen Baghs across the country.

Endnotes

[1] https://www.luther.de/en/ws.html

[2] https://www.mkgandhi.org/voiceoftruth/civildisobedience.htm

[3] https://www.africa.upenn.edu/Articles_Gen/Letter_Birmingham.html

[4] https://www.tennessean.com/story/news/2018/08/09/billy-ray-irick-execution-death-penalty-vigil/944988002/

19

Christian Discipleship: A Call to be Transformed Nonconformists
Romans 12:2

Christian vocation is to discern the call of God and to become disciples of Christ in the here and now. The discernment process of our vocation is therefore to identify our space and role in God's redemptive work in history. The discernment of God's will, informed by the signs of the times, should inspire us, and lead us to new leaps of faith. They should inspire us to dream new discipleship journeys, leaving the safety of our cocoons to an adventurous celebration of life in the company of the other. It is the commitment to become available to God in God's redemptive mission in the world, doing what God expects us to do.

The English word "vocation" is derived from the Latin word *vocatio*. *Vocare* is the root verb, meaning 'to call'. While *vocatio* (vocation) could refer to God's call to all, in the late medieval world it was increasingly connected with "religious" vocations of priests, monks and nuns which were seen as spiritually superior to "worldly" work. It is in this context that Martin Luther reaffirmed all constructive works as expressions of God's call. It was a theological move affirming the priesthood of all believers.

Our vocation, therefore, is not some special religious responsibility that is assigned to us, but something down to earth, exercised right in the world of everyday realities and struggles. Vocation, therefore, is our Christian call to live out our faith in loving and in serving our neighbours as an expression of our love towards God.

Christian discipleship therefore is the vocation to incarnate the gospel of Jesus Christ in the lives of our neighbours. And this gospel is the gospel of the redemption of the whole earth. So Christians, as Luther rightly puts it,

> should be guided in all their works by this thought and contemplate this one thing alone, that they may serve and benefit others in all that they do, considering nothing except the need and the advantage of their neighbor.[1]

Paul's epistle to the church in Rome is an exhortation to us to present our bodies as a living sacrifice and to be transformed by the renewing of our minds without conforming to the world. In our dominant understanding we tend to consider world as evil, and hence, Paul's exhortation is misinterpreted as a life apart from the world so as to remain sinless. But Paul is challenging us to come out of the prevailing success-driven worldviews of power and domination and to transform ourselves by the renewal of our minds with alternative visions and practices. We should not be preoccupied with a selfish desire to keep away from the sinful world to remain as pure and sinless; rather, our vocation is to participate in God's redeeming work of transforming the sinful world. This sense of vocation requires from us a costly commitment to offer ourselves as a living sacrifice as Jesus did.

Christian Discipleship: A Call to "Sin Boldly"

In our Christian life, we tend to be more worried about the possibility of committing sin, and hence we prefer to stay detached from the sinful world to remain sinless and godly. Here, Luther's advice to Melanchthon to "sin boldly, but believe and rejoice in Christ even more boldly"[2] is relevant to us. Since we are both saints and sinners, sin is inevitable in our life; but because of Christ we do not have to be overly conscious of the fear of doing the wrong thing. Justified by faith, we are encouraged to act, accepting the possibility of failure while trusting in Christ's victory over sin and death.

Our problem is our reluctance to "sin boldly." We do not want to get it wrong. As a result, we abstain from all social interventions and try to lead a pious and spiritual life, insulating ourselves from all the possibilities of getting contaminated by the world. This unwillingness within us to "sin boldly" is our "moral inertia" which prevents us from doing our vocation. Moral inertia disengages us from the cry of the victims. There could be many reasons for our moral inertia. First of all, we have failed in understanding the structural and systemic nature of sin, and as a result we do not perceive hunger, casteism, ecological destruction, homophobia and patriarchy as sin. We also tend to avoid and deny our participation in these systemic sins that cause death and destruction. When it comes to casteism or patriarchy, we prefer to deny their existence and abstain from discussing about it. Those who show the nerve to address these systemic evils are criticised for destroying community life. With a privatised understanding of morality, we refuse to get involved in social issues. As Rabbi Abraham Heschel reminds us, "Indifference to evil is even more evil than evil itself."

Secondly, our reluctance to "sin boldly" is also due to our denial of recognising ourselves as God's co-workers. As friends of God, we are called and empowered by God to receive God's love and live out that justice-making love in the world. We are here for a purpose: to let God work through us so that the world may experience healing, restoration and the fullness of life. This is our vocation as Christ's body on earth today. But we have failed in understanding the gospel of Christ which has set us free from sin to serve God's earth.

Thirdly, our moral inertia is also caused by our sense of powerlessness. Our fear of "not being able to make a difference" is preventing us from moral engagement. We are too conscious about sinful structures. We are also too preoccupied with success stories. Shiphrah and Puah, the two midwives of Exodus 2, are living examples for the courage to "sin boldly." They had to make a choice between Pharaoh's order and divine will. It was a morally ambiguous situation. They were not clear about the consequences of their action. But they showed the courage to act, trusting in God's promises. Christian discipleship, therefore, is a call to become transformed nonconformists. It requires the courage and commitment to "sin boldly."

Christian Discipleship: A Commitment to Creative Maladjustment

For apostle Paul, conformism is a state of being conformed to the present eon. For Paul, the present eon is a state of corruption, and hence being conformed to it is to participate in its corruptness. So, our nonconformism towards the present eon is creative as it leads to judgment, resistance and transformation. The journey of Christian discipleship is a constant struggle to pronounce "Sorry, I beg to differ" to the prevailing order in innumerable moments of our daily life. It requires courage and commitment.

Even though our churches attempt to witness to the coming eon and manifest foretastes of the coming eon in its ministries and mission, these manifestations unfortunately belong to the present eon. They enjoy sharing the corruptness of the present eon. We continue to misuse and abuse Scripture and tradition to perpetuate the prevailing sinful order. So, while we continue to be part of the church, we need to resist the temptation to be conformed to it. Nonconformity is the resistance to idolatry. It is the critique of all our attempts to absolutise ourselves, our church, our tradition, our institution, our community and our nation.

Fifty years ago, addressing a gathering at the Western Michigan University, Dr. Martin Luther King Jr. affirmed,

> Certainly, we all want to avoid the maladjusted life. In order to have real adjustment within our personalities, we all want the well-adjusted life in order to avoid neurosis, schizophrenic personalities. But I say to you, my friends, as I move to my conclusion, there are certain things in our nation and in the world which I am proud to be maladjusted and which I hope all people of good-will will be maladjusted until the good societies realize. I say very honestly that I never intend to become adjusted to segregation and discrimination. I never intend to become adjusted to religious bigotry. I never intend to adjust myself to economic conditions that will take necessities from the many to give luxuries to the few. I never intend to adjust myself to the madness of militarism, and to self-defeating effects of physical violence.[3]

In a sermon based on Romans 12: 1-2, Dr. King further elaborated the theology of creative maladjustment.

> We are called to be people of conviction, not conformity, of moral nobility not social respectability. We are commanded to live differently and according to a higher loyalty. As Christians we must never surrender our supreme loyalty to any time-bound

custom of earth-bound ideas for at the heart of our universe is a higher reality—God and God's kingdom of love to which we must be conformed. The saving of our world from pending doom will come, not through the complacent adjustment of the conforming majority but through the *creative maladjustment* of a nonconforming majority.[4]

The story of the resilience and struggle of Dongria Kondhs in Odisha to save Niyamgiri hills is one of nonconformism to protect and celebrate life. Their refusal to believe that there are no alternatives and their resolve not to be incorporated into the logic of the market is paradigmatic for us in our discipleship journey. We see similar stories of resistance and celebration in different parts of the country, inviting us to live out our Christian discipleship of creative maladjustment.

To be creatively maladjusted is an alternative worldview and behaviour, a radical departure from what is usually expected. Creative maladjustment means to be aligned with the gospel imperative to be persistent and insistent on reversing any trend towards exclusion and discrimination and to be engaged in the struggles of the marginalised and disenfranchised. Creative maladjustment means to be inclusive and to reject the purity maps and codes of the dominant worldview. Creative maladjustment, as Paul observes, is not to be conformed to this world, but to be transformed by the renewing of our minds.

Our journey of discipleship begins with the discernment of our vocation. Let us boldly proclaim that we denounce conformity to the prevailing order and that we intend to live a life of creative maladjustment. This requires the courage to identify systemic evils, to name them, to challenge them and to eradicate them by participating in the ongoing struggles of subaltern communities.

Christian vocation rejects the notion that God is a superman who fixes world's problems. Rather, Christian vocation challenges us to a radical discipleship to incarnate God's power and embodied presence in history through our courage to "sin boldly" and make creative maladjustments for the sake of life.

Endnotes

[1] Harold John Grimm and Helmut T. Lehmann (Editors). *Luther's Works #31*, (Minneapolis: Fortress Press, 1957), 364.

[2] Let Your Sins Be Strong: A Letter from Luther to Melanchthon: Letter no. 99, 1 August 1521: From Wartburg Castle (Text) http://www.ctsfw.net/media/pdfs/LutherToMelanchthon.pdf

[3] https://wmich.edu/sites/default/files/attachments/MLK.pdf

[4] https://zangodare.wordpress.com/2011/12/24/the-maladjusted-non-conformist/

Magnificat:
A Call to Become Mothers of God

Luke 1: 46-55

Mary of Nazareth is one of those biblical characters who has been mythologised and sanitised far beyond any historical likeness. Our dominant Mariology is both patriarchal and hegemonic, and it continues to legitimise male domination in the church and society by compelling women to internalise patriarchal values. For the church, Mary is the ultimate ideal of true womanhood, something akin to Sita of the Hindu scriptures, the epitome of the ideal Indian womanhood. Our Mariology continues to devalue women by valorising obedience, humility, passivity and submission as the virtues of women.

When it comes to Marian devotion, we have at least two models of Mary. The Mary of the institutionalised church is a docile virgin who was obedient to the divine will. She is portrayed as standing on a crescent moon, wearing a crown, with rings on her fingers. She has a blue robe embroidered with gold. On the other hand, the Mary of popular piety is an organic deity rooted in the everyday struggles of the people. Our Lady of

Vailankanni is known as *Arokkiya Annai*, the Holy Mother of Good Health, who brings healing in the community.

Mariology for the Catholics in Central and Latin America is connected to *Our Lady of Guadalupe*, whose image shares the features of the people of Mexico. She is seen as a benefactor of the oppressed. For the common people, the *Lady of Guadalupe* is the maternal and feminine image of the divine who heals them and liberates them. We see a similar Marian devotion during the first week of September in the streets of Bangalore when subaltern communities celebrate the feast of St. Mary at St. Mary's Basilica in Shivaji Nagar. What we find in all these Marian devotions is the appropriation of Mother Mary by the grassroots communities, contesting the Mariology of the domesticated Mary of the church.

The model of true womanhood perpetuated through the dominant Mariology of the church is detrimental to the flourishing of women as it prevents the development of their critical intellect, impairs their capacity for discernment and righteous anger, and disables their moral agency. As Simone de Beauvoir rightly observed, "The supreme victory of masculinity is consummated in Mariolatry: it signifies the rehabilitation of woman through the completeness of her defeat."[1] The exaltation of Mary in the traditional Marian devotion which places Mary on a high pedestal has always been used to denigrate women. Mary's motherhood has "legitimated domesticity as the primary vocation for women."[2] Notions of the eternal feminine, essential feminine nature and ideal womanhood that the dominant Mariology propagates are toxic for women's survival and development and hence need to be contested. It requires a new engagement with the Mary of Nazareth, and we need to enable her to speak out.

The New Testament does not give much importance to Mary—either as a historical figure or as a theological symbol. Paul does not refer to Mary by name at all. In the infancy narratives of Matthew, Joseph is the main actor, and Mary plays a passive role. However, in the Lukan infancy narratives, we see Mary the protagonist. The angelic visit comes to her. She is consulted in advance and she gives her consent. Her parents or future husband are not involved in her decisions. She is autonomous and an active agent in Luke's narrative. She travels to visit Elizabeth without taking permission from her future husband. For Luke, Mary is more than a passive instrument of God; she is an independent agent with autonomy, who participates in God's redemptive mission in history.

The memory of Mary of Nazareth can subvert our Mariological fantasies. Mary of Nazareth is not the modest and beautiful white woman of artistic imagination, kneeling before her son, acknowledging her inferiority. She is the pregnant and bold teenager, living in an occupied territory, who envisions a world devoid of imperial occupation, economic exploitation, and social exclusion. She is aware of the consequences of an unwed young girl becoming pregnant in her society. As we read in the Gospel of Matthew, Joseph was planning to cancel the wedding because he wanted to protect Mary from public humiliation and social ostracism. According to Jewish law, as an alleged adulteress, Mary could have been stoned to death.

So, it is important for us to revisit the story and listen to Mary and to discern why she gave her consent to becoming the mother of Jesus. In this search, the *Magnificat*, the song of Mary, becomes significant. Our engagement with the *Magnificat* should begin by questioning the dominant assumption that Mary, as the radiant woman and the handmaid of God, composed the *Magnificat* peacefully. The *Magnificat* belongs to the long Hebrew tradition of revolutionary songs that proclaimed God's commitment to bring about radical reversal in socioeconomic relations. When we discern Mary as a rural peasant girl who boldly sings her song of protest and alternatives, envisioning her dreams of a world without domination, injustice, marginalisation and abuse of power, Mary's song becomes a radical resource for us in the twenty-first century to live out our faith relevantly in our context.

Let us reflect upon two important questions that we normally try to avoid. First, why did God choose Mary to be the mother of Jesus? Second, why did Mary decide to become the mother of Jesus?

Why did God choose Mary to be the mother of Jesus? Mary was humble, meek and mild, and obedient to accepting God's will, even though it would lead almost definitely to a shameful fate. This is the familiar, canonised answer of the church. Through this answer the church has constructed the normative model of a true Christian woman and we all have internalised it; obedient, passive, humble and conformist. But Luke does not seem to agree with this answer. When Mary says, "My soul magnifies the Lord, and my spirit rejoices in God my saviour, for he has looked with favour on the lowliness of the servant"(Luke 1: 46-48a), she is not valorising her humility or humbleness. Rather, Mary gives us clear indications about her social location and the diverse manifestations of structural evil that she experiences because of her identity as a poor, colonised, rural, peasant woman. The Greek word for "lowliness" is *tapeinosis*, and it does not refer to any innate inner virtues or qualities such as humbleness or humility; rather it represents humiliation or unjust affliction and torture by a sinful social order. In other words, Mary here magnifies the Lord for the divine preferential option of choosing the victims of the prevailing order as partners in God's salvific mission. So, Mary does not sing the *Magnificat* as a saint or as the epitome of true womanhood, but as a fierce young woman confronting the painful experiences of exploitation and humiliation of her own concrete social location.

Yes, God has chosen Mary to be the mother of Jesus because that is the politics of God: preferential option for the victims of structural injustice and evil. Further, Luke invites us to go beyond an essentialist position here. Of course, Mary was a subaltern. But she was intentional about her subaltern experiences and she used her experiences to develop an alternative consciousness. Mary was convinced about the purpose of her life and she did not bother to get permission from her parents or the rabbi or even her future husband to become pregnant. The angelic episode reveals Mary's autonomy over her body and her life and her courage to be the subject of her life and destiny.

God chooses people who are deeply intentional about their experiences of imposed marginalisation and are committed to overthrow the systems that continue to enslave and dehumanise them. Further, we witness here the politics of God which do not agree with dominant notions and practices. We see two pregnant women in this story: an unwed teenage girl and a postmenopausal woman. The politics of God, revealed in the Lukan infancy narratives, proclaims God's favour on those who are considered illegitimate, infertile and incapable, and invites them to become mothers to give birth to a new dispensation of divine justice and love on earth.

Why did Mary decide to become the mother of Jesus? As a young, Jewish woman, Mary was familiar with the Jewish anticipation of the messiah who would bring about radical transformation in the world. She was also familiar with the Jewish tradition of songs of protest and alternatives which helped them to keep their hope alive during imperial oppression and social and economic exploitation. Those songs proclaimed their confidence in the divine promise to contest the claims of an unjust world, and lift up all those who have been oppressed. The reversal that the messiah would bring about was the dream of Mary. The angelic visitation offered Mary the possibility to play a decisive role in realising their messianic expectation, and she said yes to that call and vocation.

The *Magnificat* is the theological explanation that Mary offers us to clarify the rationale for her decision to become the mother of Jesus. Even though the church diluted the revolutionary message of Mary's song, it continues to destabilise and disrupt the prevailing order. We gather from Luke's narrative that even Jesus was deeply influenced by Mary's vision, and that is reflected in his inaugural sermon in Nazareth.

When the Anglican missionary Henry Martyn came to Calcutta as chaplain to the East India Company in 1805, he was shocked to know that the British authorities had banned the chanting of the *Magnificat* at evensong. Mary's song was banned in Argentina after the Mothers of the Disappeared placed the words of the Magnificat on posters throughout the capital plaza, calling for non-violent resistance against the military rule in mid-1970s. In the 1980s, the Guatemalan government discovered Mary's song to be too dangerous and revolutionary because it inspired the Guatemalan poor to believe that socio-economic reversal was possible. The government had no other option but to ban the public recital of the *Magnificat*. All these historical narratives prove that Mary's yes to God's invitation to become the mother of Jesus was inspired by her politics; the politics of the system-threatening reign of God.

We have tried to engage with two important questions, and our reflections on those questions lead us to a third question. How do we ourselves qualify to sing the *Magnificat* in our times? Or rather, what is our *Magnificat* for our times? Perhaps, the fourteenth century German mystic Meister Eckhart can help us respond to that question.

> What good is it to me if this eternal birth of the divine Son takes place unceasingly, but does not take place within myself? And, what good is it to me if Mary is full of grace and I am not also full of grace? What good is it to me for the Creator to give birth to his son if I do not also give birth to him in my time and my culture? This, then, is the fullness of time: when the Son of God is begotten in us. We are all meant to be mothers of God, for God is always needing to be born.[3]

We are familiar with the theological controversy over the title *theotokos* (mother of God). Some churches consider Mary as the mother of God, while for others she is only the mother of Jesus Christ. We are living in a context similar to that of the context of the young Mary of Nazareth. God is in need to be born in our context, and God wants us to become *theotokos* to continue the divine mission of reversal in our times. But in order to become mothers of God, we need to have the courage to become illegitimate to the prevailing order. As Mary of Nazareth practised through her life, we have to be "out of control" of all powers and principalities to give birth to the divine reversal in our times.

In November of 2016, at an award ceremony in which Prime Minister of India Narendra Modi was chief guest, the Editor of the Indian Express, Raj Kamal Jha, narrated an incident from the life of Ramnath Goenka, the former Editor of the paper. Goenka sacked a journalist when he heard the Chief Minister of a state tell him, "*Apka reporter bahot accha kaam kar raha hai*" [Your reporter is doing a great job]. "Criticism from a government is wonderful news for journalism. Criticism from a government is a badge of honour."[4]

How do we translate Raj Kamal Jha's observation on the vocation of journalists to our own vocations and ministries? If we get endorsements and applauses from the authorities, it is time for us to examine ourselves and mend our ways. As French philosopher Allan Badiou reminds us, "All resistance is a rupture with what is. And every rupture begins through a rupture with oneself."[5]

Jonathan Daniels was an Episcopal seminarian doing his Master of Divinity studies at the Episcopal Theological Seminary in Cambridge, Massachusetts, preparing himself for ordained ministry in the Episcopal Church. One evening while attending the evensong at the seminary chapel, he heard the *Magnificat* in a new and different way. When he walked out of the seminary chapel that night, he decided to leave the seminary and join the Civil Rights Movement and work along with Dr. Martin Luther King Jr. to realise the dream of reversal that the *Magnificat* proclaims. He went to Alabama to assist with voter registration, and finally ended up being killed as he lived out Mary's words.

We, as a 'called-out' community, are commissioned to bear the hope of the world in our bodies. We are called to be the containers for God to sow the seeds of hope, justice for the downtrodden and new life for the world. It is an invitation to rethink our call and to engage in the mission of the *Magnificat*. Can we feel the stirring of new life within us? Of the impossible longing to become possible? "We are all meant to be mothers of God. For God is always needing to be born."

Endnotes

[1] https://www.ewtn.com/catholicism/library/mother-of-god-or-domesticated-goddess-mary-in-feminist-theology-5688

[2] https://www.crisismagazine.com/1989/reconsidering-mary-feminist-criticism-deserves-a-response

[3] https://www.paulvasile.com/blog/2015/12/23/we-are-all-meant-to-be-mothers-of-god

[4] https://www.dailyo.in/politics/raj-kamal-jha-editor-indian-express-ramnath-goenka-awards-pm-narendra-modi-criticism-government-speech/story/1/13823.html

[5] https://hyperallergic.com/55080/are-residencies-relevant-an-exploration-in-nature/

Called to be Troublemakers

1 Kings 18:17, Matthew 10: 34-39

We live in desperate times, and our times require subversive saints and disciples who have the commitment and conviction to turn the world upside down. We are surrounded by a host of witnesses who have had the nerve to live out their faith in desperate times. Oscar Romero is one such witness, who was canonised as saint by Pope Francis on 14 October 2018, after 38 years of his martyrdom.

The term "breach" is used in English language both as a noun and a verb. As noun, it signifies an act of breaking or failing to observe a law or a code of conduct. Transgression, rupture, trespass… these are some of the synonyms for breach that we come across in dictionaries. As verb, 'breach' refers to a 'break through' or 'burst through'. For example, to break through a barrier or to make a breach. Well, what are the antonyms for breach? Obey, observe, comply with, and conform to. So, standing in the breach is a call to step into the breach. As we read in the book of Ezekiel 22:30, YHWH is searching for a person who would build up the wall and stand in the breach. There are commandments, moral codes, and community values that are breached, and we are called to stand in the breach to bring about healing, reconciliation and restoration. "Standing in the breach" is therefore proposed as a prophetic vocation for us in the context of breaches. The life and witness of Oscar Romero invites us to relook at this call to stand in the breach and to engage in alternative expressions of prophetic witness in our times. This reflection is an attempt in that direction, drawing inspiration from the teachings of Jesus and the life and witness of Saint Oscar Romero.

When Oscar Romero became archbishop of El Salvador, the country was controlled and ruled by an oligarchy which supported the economic and geopolitical interests of the United States of America. Under that repressive regime, hundreds of thousands of people simply disappeared and hundreds were killed by the militia. Since El Salvador was a largely Catholic nation, Archbishop Romero realised that his vocation was to stand in the breach and initiate peace and reconciliation between the rich and the poor, and the powerful leaders and the powerless victims. All of them were members of his church. There were also priests, nuns and members of the laity who were inspired by the teachings of Jesus and the vision of the base Christian communities developed by Vatican II and the liberation theology movement. Their understanding of Christian discipleship led them to the streets to involve themselves in active resistance against state fascism and tyranny. In that process the street became the sanctuary, and *ekklesia* happened where people gathered together to boldly proclaim "enough is enough."

It is in this context that he was handpicked by Rome, hoping that as a professor of theology, he would choose the middle path and stand in the breach without creating new breaches. Initially, he lived up to the expectations of the Vatican, and he was a strong critique of the radical clergy and laity who were fighting against the government. He also tried to change the minds and hearts of his folks who ruled the country and led the military. But soon Romero realised that the mission of the church is not to stand in the breach, but it is to create breaches. The streets of San Salvador facilitated this Damascus experience in Romero's life, and this is how he articulated it: "There is no dichotomy between human and God's image. Whoever tortures a human being, whoever abuses a human being, whoever outrages a human being, abuses God's image." This experience of epiphany, encountering God in the tortured and crucified people, anointed and empowered Romero to reimagine prophetic vocation as creating breaches. This is how his conversion experience changed his understanding of the mission of the church.

> A church that suffers no persecution but enjoys the privileges and support of the things of the earth—beware!—is not the true church of Jesus Christ. A preaching that does not point out sin is not the preaching of the gospel. A preaching that makes sinners feel good, so that they are secured in their sinful state, betrays the gospel's call.[1]

The Lukan text shares a similar insight. "I did not come to bring peace, but I came to bring a sword" (Matt 10:34). Of course, it is hard for us to comprehend such a statement from the Prince of Peace. But for Jesus, peace was not the maintenance of the status quo. It was not the absence of tension and conflict. It was not bringing premature reconciliation. Jesus was born during a time of "peace," the *Pax Romana*, Roman Peace, which existed only because Rome was able to repress all dissent. Under *Pax Romana*, everything appeared peaceful. In the context of imperial and fascist peace that is prevalent in our nations, churches, institutions and even our own families, "standing in the breach" can distort and reduce our understanding of vocation to that of a cheerleader for the system that reinforces the prevailing unjust social order. Instead of confessing and witnessing Jesus, the troublemaker, we offer a sanitised, deodorised and neutralised Christ, who will not disrupt the status quo. If we do not shift from standing in the breach to creating breaches, the system will absorb us, co-opt us and appoint us as its priests and chaplains even without our knowledge. In the end, we will continue to serve the "peaceful" system by standing in the breach.

Pax Romana continued to flourish in the Roman colonies by silencing the voices of dissent with the cross and oppressive taxation. But one night, angels shattered the repressed silence with joyful songs of "Peace on Earth!" They announced a different kind of peace to an oppressed people: The Prince of Peace had breached into history in the shape of a baby born to a poor, working-class family in an insignificant corner, far from the seats of imperial and religious power. As we read in the Gospel of Matthew, Jerusalem was terrified by the angelic proclamation of peace. And Jesus' public ministry was a consistent attempt to create breaches exposing the pseudo peace of the prevailing order.

From the streets of El Salvador, Oscar Romero realised that his vocation was not to stand in the breach and to fix the breach of trust, the breach of peace, and the breach of morality that existed in his society. For him, the faith imperative was to expose the sinfulness of the prevailing peace, trust and morality and to intentionally disrupt them. In his last sermon, he appealed to the soldiers:

> Brothers, you came from our own people. You are killing your own brothers. Any human order to kill must be subordinate to the law of God, which says, 'Thou shalt not kill.' No soldier is obliged to obey an order contrary to the law of God. No one

has to obey an immoral law. It is high time you obeyed your conscience rather than sinful orders. The church cannot remain silent before such an abomination…. In the name of God, in the name of this suffering people whose cry rises to heaven more loudly each day, I implore you, I beg you, I order you: stop the repression.[2]

What we find here is a daring call to breach the moral order and codes of conduct of a sinful system. He instigated his folks to disobey the unjust orders of the powers that be. He even called unjust rules, regulations and moral codes as abomination. This is the prophetic vocation of the church; to pronounce divine judgment on the prevailing order and to create breaches that will disrupt the functioning of sinful systems and structures. Even as we celebrate Oscar Romero's life and witness, he reminds us that in the context of systemic injustice we are called to incarnate the provocative and subversive gospel of Christ by creating breaches.

In the Hebrew Bible we read how King Ahab addressed Prophet Elijah: "You, the troublemaker of Israel" (1 Kings 18:17). If we are reluctant to accept the title of 'troublemaker,' we are not qualified to be a disciple of Jesus. In our times, if we are not known as the troublemakers of nations, the troublemakers of our churches, and the troublemakers of our institutions, we need to sit in ashes and introspect. This is the context in which we need to turn our attention to Jesus' words, "Whoever does not take up the cross and follow me is not worthy of me. Those who find their life will lose it and those who lose their life for my sake will find it" (Matt 10: 38-39).

Jesus' invitation to his followers to take up their cross and follow him was made before he was crucified. Cross was not yet a religious symbol then, but the most brutal form of death penalty imposed by the Roman Empire. So, Jesus' invitation to discipleship is to cast aside our social status and reputation and to opt for an alternative existence without social legitimacy. How different would the church look like if we understood that our basic vocation is to be illegitimate? *Ekklesia* happens in our communities when we show the nerve to become illegitimate to the prevailing order.

Oscar Romero prepared his church to be an illegitimate movement in the Salvadorian society for the cause of the gospel of Christ.

> A church that does not provoke any crisis, preach a gospel that does not unsettle, proclaim a word of God that does not get under anyone's skin or a word of God that does not touch the real sin of the society in which it is being proclaimed: what kind of gospel is that?[3]

This is how he challenged his church to rethink its mission and vocation to engage in creating breaches in society. Romero passionately called his people to become a cruciform church for the sake of the crucified people:

> If some day they take the radio station away from us, if they close down our newspaper, if they don't let us speak, if they kill all the priests and the bishop too, and you are left, a people without priests, each one of you must be God's microphone, each one of you must be a messenger, a prophet. The church will always exist as long as there is one baptized person. And that one baptized person who is left in the world is responsible before the world for holding aloft the banner of the Lord's truth and of his divine justice.[4]

Desperate times require subversive disciples and prophets. Through their lives and witnesses the cloud of witnesses inspire and invite us to continue this prophetic tradition of creating breaches for the sake of the world. Each generation requires blessed troublemakers. "Those who find their life will lose it, and those who lose their life for my sake will find it" (Matt 10: 39).

Endnotes

[1] http://www.catholic365.com/article/9655/a-church-that-doesnt-provoke-any-crises-a-gospel-that-doesnt-unsettle-a-word-of-god-that-doesnt-get-under-anyones-skin-a-word-of-god-that-doesnt-touc.html

[2] https://theopoet4camp.blogspot.com/2010/03/presente-remembering-romero.html

[3] http://www.catholic365.com/article/8815/a-church-that-does-not-provoke-any-crisis-preach-a-gospel-that-does-not-unsettle-proclaim-a-word-of-god-that-does-not-get-under-anyones-skin-or-a-wor.html

[4] https://sjb.hwcdsb.ca/270112--Student-leaders-called-to-Be-Gods-Microphone

Afterword

*Sunil Caleb**

The 21 biblical reflections that George Zachariah has written in this book are all powerful reminders to us who try to follow the Lord Jesus Christ as his disciples, that we cannot allow our faith in Him as the Son of God and the Saviour of the World to just be confined to our daily prayers, and weekly services or cottage-prayer meetings. As the Lord Jesus came to inaugurate the Reign of God or the "Kin[g]dom of God," we have to measure our Christian discipleship by the extent to which we are using whatever talents, time and treasure God has given us for bringing closer the Rule of God in all areas of our national and community life. Working for Justice and Liberation for all who are marginalised and oppressed is an essential part of our mission and work as Christians and these 21 reflections, each based on a particular biblical text, will give us the spiritual grounding to carry out our responsibilities towards the establishment of the "Kin[g]dom of God. These 21 reflections will act as resources which we have to adapt to our particular contexts. It will not do to just preach/proclaim them word for word as they are published here. We have to use them as a base and something that gives us background ideas which we can build on and use to speak to our own particular situations and contexts in order to proclaim the transforming Good News; Good News that will bring a Spirit of Joy and Celebration which is God's desire for the whole of creation.

The Word of God as proclaimed in these 21 reflections seeks to provoke the kind of "disturbance" that God requires in the exploitative 'status quo'. The 'normal' ways of doing things in the social and economic areas of the world today are both Unjust and Unsustainable. Inequality, both within nations and across nations, has reached gargantuan proportions, which is completely against the will and purpose of God who loves each human being and each part of the cosmos which God has so lovingly created. We have to thus, begin to move out of our comfort zones and be brave in challenging the 'powers that be' which have a vested interest in the continuation of the 'status quo'. It is risky business challenging vested interests that want the 'status quo' to continue for when we challenge vested interests we are challenging the Profits, Power and Position that men (it is usually men and so I deliberately use the male pronoun) have unjustly and through exploitative methods accumulated, dispossessing those who are socially, physically and economically weak. However, if we are true and loyal followers of our Lord Jesus Christ, then we will embark upon this 'risky business' for that is precisely what he did, challenging the powerful elite which controlled the Temple at Jerusalem in his day. As Jesus disturbed the status quo in his day by 'cleansing' the Temple we too must do the same in our churches, societies and economies. It is this work that will result in the coming of the "kin[g]dom of God."

Prayer (so that we are aligned with the Will of God) and Action (to implement the Will of God) must be in a symbiotic and complementary relationship. Just armchair theologising is not good enough. There has to be Engagement with what God is doing in the world today. This involves Discernment of what are the Emphases and Priorities of God in the world today followed by a Determination to be actively involved in carrying out the Will of God in whatever way God has set before us.

This Action to work toward the arrival on earth of the 'kin[g]dom' of God is something that not only Christians are involved in. In fact, there are perhaps more People of Faith (PoF) in other religious and atheistic traditions who are just as involved as we Christians are. What motivates such other People of Faith is a topic of interest but not the most important thing. The most important thing is for us to join hands with PoF in seeking creative ways of protest against and action to defeat the forces of Death and Destruction. We thus have to work with ALL people of goodwill, treating them with the respect that is due to those created in the image and likeness of God. The work must be creative, and involves trying to think of ways of bringing justice, hope and holistic healing to those who need it. This will, therefore, require an interdisciplinary approach where social sciences, psychology, political theory, biblical hermeneutics, appropriate technology, prayer and praise and so on are all used in order to bring succour to those in need. These various disciplines will need to be harnessed in a coordinated and cooperative manner to bring their various inputs to countering injustice and furthering Love and Justice.

The 21 reflections in this book will give us the theory, the Theology needed to be active, but they will have been read in vain if they are not used to inspire people to carry out the works of Love and Justice that they call us to perform. Our aim in life must not only be to understand the world but to transform it into the 'kin[g]dom of God' as God would have us do. While this work might seem impossible given the Powers and Principalities of Evil and Empire ranged against us, our Christian faith assures us that God's power is manifest in us in our weaknesses (I Cor. 12:9). It is when we set out in faith, giving all that we have into God's hands, that we find the strength, guidance and help needed to go forward boldly to carry out the will of God. I pray to God the Holy Spirit, the one that stands in solidarity beside us and guides us when we ask for guidance, that these 21 reflections may be a blessing to each reader and to all those who are impacted and influenced by the inspired readers.

Endnote

* **The Rev. Dr. Sunil Caleb** serves the Bishop's College, Kolkata as Principal and Professor of Christian Theology and Christian Ethics.